CAPTAIN P J RUSSELL

SEA SIGNALLING SIMPLIFIED

A manual of instruction for the
new International Code of Signals

FOURTH EDITION

Adlard Coles Ltd   London

Granada Publishing Limited
First published in the Bosun Series in 1952 and 1959
Third edition published in Great Britain 1969
by Adlard Coles Limited
Frogmore St Albans Herts AL2 2NF and
3 Upper James Street London W1R 4BP
Reprinted 1970
Fourth edition 1976

ISBN 0 229 11554 3   1760l

Printed in Great Britain by
Fletcher & Son Ltd, Norwich

623·85612

E

SEA SIGNALLING SIMPLIFIED

To Betty

ACKNOWLEDGEMENT

The Alphabetical Flags and Numeral Pendants reproduced in colour, and the various signal letters in this book are reproduced from the International Code of Signals by kind permission of the Controller of H.M. Stationery Office.

SEMAPHORE

ANSWERING
SIGN

A B C D E

F G H I J

K L M N O

P Q R S T

U V W X Y

Z ATTENTION BREAK

CONTENTS

INTRODUCTION

The notes of which this book is composed and the order in which they are set out are based on the experience gained from instructing in the old International Code of Signals since it first came into use in 1934. The book is designed to simplify the teaching and learning of the new International Code either in classes or in self tuition.

Being of pocket size, it enables those who either seldom use the Code or have only a slight knowledge of it, to carry it with them and to signal correctly at any time, without difficulty, by referring to the Index.

PRELIMINARY INSTRUCTION

The lists of Distress Signals, International Sanitary Regulations (Pratique Messages), Radiotelephone Procedure for use in distress and the Table of Life Saving Signals have been placed on pages 75–84 for easy reference in cases of emergency.

Being self explanatory they do not require instruction but it is advisable for the reader to become familiar with them.

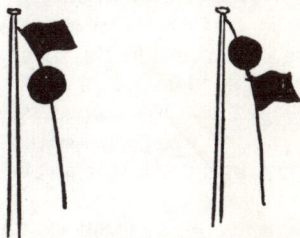

Fig. 1

It is worth remembering that Distress Signal 7, see Fig. 1 could be made by a shirt and a bucket if other means are not available. Radiotelephone Distress Procedure will be more easily understood after completing the instruction given on Radiotelephony.

Signalling is a fascinating pastime and those learning it will find that their interest will increase with their knowledge.

9

At sea it is the method by which ships of all nationalities talk to each other.

The revised International Code of Signals with which this book is concerned is a universal language which they use.

It is printed in English, French, Italian, German, Japanese, Spanish, Norwegian, Russian and Greek.

It is referred to as the revised International Code of Signals as some of the previous Code has been retained, although it differs fundamentally from the Code which came into use in 1934.

The principle of this new Code, which came into operation on 1 April 1969, is that each signal has a complete meaning.

The Code is contrived primarily for the safety of navigation and persons especially when language difficulties arise.

It can be transmitted by all forms of communication including radiotelephony and radiotelegraphy.

Account has also been taken of the fact that the wide use of radiotelephony and radiotelegraphy can provide simple and effective means of communication, in plain language, whenever language difficulties do not exist.

Eight methods are employed at sea for conveying signals:
1. Flag signalling, which means the flying of the different coloured flags and pendants of the International Code.
2. Flashing-light signalling, by which messages are conveyed by lamp using the dots and dashes of the Morse code.
3. Radiotelegraphy, using the Morse code and commonly called buzzer.
4. Sound signalling, by which messages are sent by Morse code, using whistle, siren, foghorn etc.
5. Morse signalling using hand-flags or arms to make the dots and dashes.
6. The Semaphore code, made by movements of the arms with or without hand-flags.
7. The voice, using a loud hailer.
8. The voice, using radiotelephony.

The object of any signalling is to get a message delivered accurately in the least possible time and by the most convenient means.

It follows naturally that when a signal has to be made the appropriate medium, from the eight methods described, is selected. For example, it would be absurd to hoist flags and pendants if the message could be delivered more easily by using a loud hailer. The best advice which can be given to those wishing to learn the International Code of Signals is to study the subject in the order in which this book is written and strictly according to the instructions contained in it. The sequence has been carefully thought out and is based on many years experience in instructing.

Before any progress can be made in actual signalling it is necessary for the beginner to commit to memory the flags and pendants of the International Code, the Morse code, the Semaphore code and the Phonetic Tables.

The object of introducing these at this stage is to enable the student to practise sending and receiving the letters and figures from the beginning and thus becoming familiar with these codes as instruction progresses.

Further, by teaching them what might be described as the drudgery of signalling has been completed and the remaining study is made more interesting.

Learning the procedures for these different methods of communication, without which practical signalling cannot be properly conducted, will then be easy.

2

INTERNATIONAL CODE FLAGS
AND PENDANTS

If the reader will turn to the coloured page of flags and pendants on the endpapers he will see that each letter of the alphabet is represented by a flag; these twenty-six flags are known as the Alphabetical Flags.

Each number from one to nought is shown by a pendant; these are called the Numeral Pendants.

Next we have the triangular flags referred to as Substitutes and last, but not least, a pendant described as the Code and Answering Pendant.

It is necessary for the reader to get to know all the flags and pendants by sight so well that each can be recognized at a glance. Learning to recognize these flags will not prove so difficult as may appear at first sight.

The coloured page on the back endpaper is a duplicate of the page at the beginning of the book and the student is advised to cut out the duplicate page now and then cut out each flag and pendant separately, sticking or writing the letter or number on the back, and keeping the whole set in a match box or envelope. By shuffling the set together, as one would dominoes and selecting each flag from memory rapid progress will be made. For example, it is desired to choose the flag which represents the letter Q. Search among the jumble of flags on the table before you for the plain yellow flag and you have it.

The flags and pendants have been very carefully designed

and in most cases a flag or pendant can be recognized if only a part of it is visible.

Various aids to memory can be devised. For instance, take the flag which stands for the letter I. This is a yellow flag with a black ball in the centre, the colours and design somewhat resembling a black eye. The letters A and B are very easy to remember as they are the only two burgees in the Code and B is the red burgee. Later on these cut-out flags will be found invaluable for making up the signals given as examples under the headings in the chapter on flag and pendant signalling.

THE MORSE CODE

In the Morse code each letter of the alphabet is represented by one or more dots or dashes or a combination of them. Letters are recognized in Morse signalling by the arrangement of the dots and dashes. In practice this is less difficult than it sounds.

At sea, the signal lamp is the official and most suitable method used for transmitting visual Morse messages.

A signal lamp can be anything from an electric torch to a searchlight. An oil lamp, with a dioptric lens, is manufactured for the purpose. There are also electric masthead lights run off the ship's power, which are visible all round the horizon. A very efficient modern type of lamp, called the Aldis lamp, resembles a motor car headlight except that it is cylindrical in form. It is held in the hand and the light is directed towards the distant ship by means of sights, usually of the aperture variety. As the lamp is held in the hand, it can be kept focused on the receiving ship by moving it to compensate for the rolling and pitching of the transmitting ship. Signals are made by pressing a trigger which deflects the reflector.

The range of signal lamps varies considerably according to the power, size and type, the minimum being between two and three miles at night. Powerful modern electric signalling lamps can also be used by day. A small lamp of this kind can be seen at approximately two miles by day and six miles by night, with the naked eye. With a telescope it is visible from three to four miles by day and up to twelve miles at night. Larger sizes can be read easily up to eight miles by day.

A signal lamp should be isolated from other lights as far as possible. This is especially important where there are lights which appear to go on and off because people are walking in front of them, or where the lights are caused by traffic passing to and fro on a quayside or a road alongside a harbour.

THE MORSE CODE

Letters		*Letters*		*Numerals*	
A	·—	N	—·	1	·————
B	—···	O	———	2	··———
C	—·—·	P	·——·	3	···——
D	—··	Q	——·—	4	····—
E	·	R	·—·	5	·····
F	··—·	S	···	6	—····
G	——·	T	—	7	——···
H	····	U	··—	8	———··
I	··	V	···—	9	————·
J	·———	W	·——	0	—————
K	—·—	X	—··—		
L	·—··	Y	—·——		
M	——	Z	——··		

PROCEDURE SIGNALS

$\overline{AR}$	·—·—·	End of message.
$\overline{AS}$	·—···	Waiting signal.
$\overline{AAA}$	·—·—·—	Full stop or decimal point.

Bar over the top of the letters means they should be run together and made as one symbol.

Note Certain letters such as 'è' 'ä' 'ö' etc., have been omitted from this list of Morse Symbols because:

14

(a) they are not to be used internationally; (b) they are contained in local codes and (c) some of them can be substituted by a combination of two letters.

There are some who learn the Morse Code by beginning with the letter **A** and proceeding doggedly through to **Z**.

There is an easier system than this. Begin by learning the letters composed solely of dashes, **T**, **M**, **O**, and then those which are all dots **E**, **I**, **S**, **H**. This should take about ten minutes, by which time one-third of the alphabet will have been committed to memory. Next memorize those beginning with dots and ending in one dash **A**, **U**, **V**, and then those beginning with one dash and ending with dots, **N**, **D**, **B**. The remaining letters should then be learnt by heart. When the letters of the alphabet have been mastered the numbers 1 to 0 can be tackled followed by the Procedure signals.

These will be found to be comparatively easy.

SPACING

It is most essential that spacing in Morse should be correct, as attention to this makes all the difference between good and bad sending and easy or difficult reading. By 'spacing' is meant the length of a dot as compared to that of a dash, the interval of time between each dot and dash, and the time between each letter in a word and each word in a message.

Officially, a dot is one unit, and a dash three units. A dash is always, therefore, three times as long as a dot. The pause between each dot and dash in a letter is one unit: between each letter it is three units, between two words or groups it is equivalent to seven units.

Naturally the spaces and lengths of dots and dashes vary according to the rate of sending but they are invariably the same in proportion to the rate and to one another. The ratio must always be maintained. In actual practice, the important points to remember are that a dash is three times longer than a dot, that there is a slight pause between each letter and that there is a longer pause between each word. It is also advisable to make the dots very slightly shorter in proportion so as to accentuate the difference between a dot and a dash.

RATES OF SENDING

Before making the first attempt to use a Morse key, the reader should understand something about Morse rates, or, in other words, the speed of sending.

The following is the method by which a Morse rate is arrived at. For the purposes of rate assessment, a Morse word is assumed to consist of five letters. Thus, in a plain language message, the letters are counted and divided by five. In this way a message of three words, containing a total of ten letters, would be reckoned as two groups and if this was sent in exactly one minute the rate of sending would be two words a minute.

The standard rate of signalling by flashing light in the revised code is forty letters a minute which is equivalent to a rate of eight words a minute.

MORSE PRACTICE

Small signalling sets for practice purposes are obtainable. They consist of a Morse key on top of a box which contains a small dry battery, a Morse armature buzzer and a lamp made up of a bull's-eye and an electric torch bulb. There is a switch to enable the operator to change from buzzer to lamp at will.

Anyone of an electrical turn of mind could construct a signal lamp for practising Morse, by simply connecting a Morse key to an electric torch bulb and small dry battery. In fact an electric torch of the press button type could be used if nothing else was available. However, the reader is advised to acquire a proper Morse key and a few words on the correct way to use it will be of help.

At one end of it will be found a screw by which the beat (actual movement which the key makes during operation) can be regulated and it is best not to have too wide a gap between the key and the contact. For fast rates, a small gap is recommended, but it is better not to have too fine a gap for lamp signalling.

The knob should be held with the first and second fingers on top and the thumb underneath. The remaining two fingers are not used. It is important to hold the key lightly and work the key from the wrist, leaving the arm and fore-arm slack. Gripping the key tightly and keeping the arm taut is totally unnecessary and will soon result in cramp or discomfort.

It is best to learn Morse with another person. In lamp practice, the ideal arrangement is to have a third person to write down each letter as it is called out by the reader. If this is not practicable, many ways will occur to the reader of managing without a 'writer down'. One method is to have two lamps and to hold conversations in Morse across a room or table. This is also an excellent way to learn Morse Procedure, as each individual can signal as if from a separate ship, all the rules being correctly observed. Learning lamp signalling according to the International Morse Code procedure in this manner can, in fact, become quite an interesting indoor game. For those who have to learn entirely by themselves it is possible to get to recognize the different letters by signalling into a mirror and watching the reflection. Speed in Morse signalling comes only with practice and it is best to begin at a very slow rate and gradually increase the speed as proficiency is attained.

It is strongly recommended that to begin with messages should be in the form of five-letter and figure Code groups or alternatively five-letter code group messages and five-figure group messages.

Example: **XLV4J**
YOJQS
39571

These can be made up to include all the numerals and letters of the alphabet. By reading groups of this type the beginner cannot do any guessing and gets into the good habit of reading automatically each letter as it is sent. When reading plain language there is a strong and natural tendency to guess the word after reading the first few letters. This should be emphatically discouraged in actual signalling, as serious mistakes can be made.

During learning, a message should be checked with the original when it has been received and all letters which are wrong should be crossed out. If the student marks each message in this fashion, judgement of the progress made will be possible and as mistakes become infrequent the rate of sending may be increased. For example, if messages can be read accurately at three words a minute, the time has come to increase the rate to four words a minute.

Marking messages has another advantage. It enables the operator to discover the letters which are found to be difficult. These vary with each individual. When it becomes apparent that a person keeps making the same mistakes with certain letters, groups of these letters can be made up and sent repeatedly until they are read correctly.

Bear in mind that everyone can send faster than they can receive.

THE SEMAPHORE CODE

Semaphore provides a quick and simple means of transmitting messages. For short distances it is excellent, but it is not suitable for long range signalling and, of course, it cannot be used at night.

The reader will discover on pages 4 and 20 that each letter is made by a different position of the arms or arm. As each movement spells a letter it is faster than Morse, which may require up to four symbols for a letter.

Semaphore can be made with the arms alone but it is obvious that by using semaphore flags the signals are more distinct and can be read farther away. It is important to hold the flag poles so that they are always in a straight line with the arms, which should never be bent when making a letter. To make the angles correctly is also very essential.

If this is not done the receiver of the signal will not be able to distinguish between **A** and **B**, **R**, **U** and **Q**, or **K** and **L** to take just a few examples.

Shore stations and big ships can be equipped with mechanical semaphores and with these the arm angles are invariably correct.

Each word starts from the *break* position shown in the Figures and at the end of each word the arms are brought down to the *break* position.

When the same two letters have to be sent following each other, as, for example, in the word 'keel' the arms are brought down to the *break* position after the first e and the next e is made immediately afterwards without pausing. In letters made with one arm, the arm not in use remains at the *break* position.

When signalling in semaphore the sender always faces the receiving ship. Thus every letter appears in reverse to the reader. The letter **A**, for instance, is made with the right arm but when receiving a message the sender's right arm (as he is facing the receiver), will be seen by the receiver on his own left hand.

The skyline makes a good background for semaphore, especially if the sender is in silhouette or wearing dark clothing.

It is very easy to learn semaphore and the beginner will find little difficulty in remembering the correct position for the arms in each letter.

As in Morse, it is easier to learn with a class or with another person. Two people facing each other across a room can practise by conversing in semaphore.

For those who have to learn single-handed, sets of cards can be obtained, each card being a picture of a sender as he appears to the receiver when making a letter, with the letter printed on the back. These can be shuffled like playing cards and each letter read in turn. By using one of these sets valuable experience in reading can be gained.

It must be remembered that the International Code semaphore (Fig. 2, page 20) differs from the original

INTERNATIONAL CODE SEMOPHORE

Fig. 2

NOTE: In order to illustrate some common faults which the student should take great care to avoid, certain letters in the drawings on this page are shown as examples of bad sending. In D,J,K,P,T,V, the arm held above the head is bent, whereas it should be straight; the angle of the arm held across the body in H and I is imperfect and compares unfavourably with that in X and Z, for instance, the two latter being correct.

code in the formation of the letters, **H, I, O, W, X, Z,** by reversing the arm position.

When learning the International Code for examination purposes it would be best to learn and use the International Code method of making these letters.

The original Semaphore Code is still in use and can be seen on page 4. For practical signalling it gives the best silhouette.

PHONETIC TABLES

It is now advisable to learn the Phonetic Tables used in radiotelephony and voice transmission. (See Table 1, pages 78 and 79.)

The advantage gained by learning these tables at this time is obvious. By so doing the phonetic pronunciation can be used as required when referring to letters and figures in other forms of signalling. These tables will thus be kept constantly in mind.

DEFINITIONS

Almost every subject has its own official jargon. The technical terms used in signalling are known, in the International Code, as *Definitions*.

The following list and their meanings should be memorized as they will be referred to frequently in the course of instruction:

Addressee is the authority to whom a signal is addressed.

Group denotes one or more continuous letter and/or numeral which together compose a signal.

A Hoist consists of one or more groups displayed from a single halyard. A hoist or signal is said to be *at the dip* when it is hoisted about half of the full extent of the halyards. A hoist or signal is said to be *close up* when it is hoisted to the full extent of the halyards.

Identity signal or *call sign* is the group of letters and figures assigned to each station by its administration.

A numeral group consists of one or more numerals.

Originator is the authority who orders a signal to be sent.

Procedure denotes the rules drawn up for the conduct of signalling.

Procedure signal is a signal designed to facilitate the conduct of signalling (see pages 24–25).

Receiving station is the station by which a signal is actually being read.

Sound signalling is any method of passing Morse signals by means of siren, whistle, foghorn, bell, or other sound apparatus.

Station means a ship, aircraft, survival craft or any place at which communications can be effected by any means.

Station of destination is that station in which the signal is finally received by the addressee.

Station of origin is that station where the originator hands in a signal for transmission irrespective of the method of communication employed.

Tackline is a length of halyard about six feet (2 m) long used to separate each group of flags.

Time of origin is the time at which a signal is ordered to be made.

Transmitting station is the station by which a signal is actually being made.

Visual signalling is any method of communication, the transmission of which is capable of being seen.

PROCEDURE SIGNALS

Procedure signals can be defined as recognized signals used in signalling by the transmitting or receiving stations to facilitate the sending or receiving of messages.

There is a proper time and place for each Procedure Signal and this conforms to its meaning and purpose.

Only when the reader has memorized all these signals, learnt their meanings and the correct method of using them has he qualified to carry out actual signalling.

The reason for this is that, in practice, Procedure Signals will be found to occur, frequently.

Each form of signalling has a few Procedure Signals peculiar to itself and these will be learnt when dealing with the various methods later.

In addition the revised International Code also gives a list of Procedure Signals for use where appropriate, in all forms of transmission.

Most of these signals appear to be self explanatory but

an explanation of their uses will be found to be of assistance and will also give an insight into signalling in general.

Before beginning instruction on this subject the reader should be informed that common sense plays a great part in practical signalling. Always put yourself in the position of the other ship and remember that she is trying, either to receive your message correctly, to send her message without mistakes or to understand what you require from her. Consequently, use your Procedure Signals to these ends and in a way which avoids ambiguity and leaves no doubt as to your meaning.

SIGNALS FOR USE WHERE APPROPRIATE IN ALL FORMS OF TRANSMISSION

AA *All after* . . . (used after the 'Repeat signal' **(RPT)**) means *Repeat all after* . . .

AB *All before* . . . (used after the 'Repeat signal' **(RPT)**) means *Repeat all before* . . .

$\overline{\text{AR}}$ Ending signal or End of Transmission or signal.

$\overline{\text{AS}}$ Waiting signal or period.

BN *All between* . . . *and* . . . (used after the 'Repeat signal' **(RPT)**) means *Repeat all between* . . . *and* . . .

C Affirmative—**YES** or *The significance of the previous group should be read in the affirmative.*

CS *What is the name or identity signal of your vessel (or station)?*

DE *From* . . . (used to precede the name or identity signal of the calling station).

K *I wish to communicate with you* or *Invitation to transmit.*

NO Negative—**NO** or *the significance of the previous group should be read in the negative.* When used in voice transmission the pronunciation should be **NO.**

OK Acknowledging a correct repetition or *It is correct.*

RQ Interrogative, or, *The significance of the previous group should be read as a question.*

R *Received* or *I have received your last signal.*

24

RPT Repeat signal *I repeat* or *Repeat what you have sent* or *Repeat what you have received*.
WA *Word or group after* . . . (used after the 'Repeat signal' **(RPT)**) means *Repeat word or group after* . . .
WB *Word or group before* . . . (used after the 'Repeat signal' **(RPT)**) means *Repeat word or group before* . . .

When **RPT** is sent by the transmitting ship or station it means that a repetition is being sent and if so the repetition *should follow immediately*.

When sent *singly* by the transmitting ship it is a request to the receiving ship to repeat back what she has received.

If **RPT** is sent by the receiving ship or station the transmitting ship should repeat back what she has sent. Another use of the signal **RPT** by either the transmitting or receiving ship could be, in the case of a very urgent or important message, to ensure that it had been received correctly.

The repeat signal must also be used, as a separate group, before the following Procedure Signals asking for corrections.

AA *All after*
AB *All before*
BN *All between*
WA *Word or group after*
WB *Word or group before*

These signals would normally be used by the receiving ship after the transmitting ship had finished the message.

The receiving ship having read the message she has received realizes that she has either not read, has read incorrectly or is doubtful of a word or words.

For example take the message:
You should keep a look out for mines.

The receiving ship finds that the words she has read after *look* do not make sense or she wants to make sure she has read them correctly.

25

She would then make the signal **RPT AA look** as three groups.

For the same reasons she might want the word after *for* and would send the signal **RPT WA for** or the words *keep a look* then the signal for the repetition would be **RPT BN should out.**

The alternatives of **WA** or **WB** and **AA** or **AB** are necessary as the same word may occur more than once in a message. In such cases care should be taken to use the proper signal to get the correction required.

OK IT IS CORRECT

This signal should be used to acknowledge a correct repetition by either the receiving or transmitting ship. **OK** can also be used as an affirmative answer to a question.

$\overline{\text{AR}}$ End of message or signal.

The bar across the top of the letters indicates that they should be run together. This applies especially in Morse sending when the letters, instead of being sent as two separate letters, are joined together as one group, thus: ■ ▬ ■ ▬ ■

$\overline{\text{AR}}$ as a separate group is always used at the end of a message by the transmitting ship after the last group has been acknowledged by the receiving ship, except in flag and pendant signalling.

It signifies the end of the message. It can also be used to mean that any transmission has ended.

For example: **RPT WA** *look* $\overline{\text{AR}}$.

R RECEIVED

R is invariably used to acknowledge $\overline{\text{AR}}$.

$\overline{\text{AS}}$ ■ ▬ ■ ■ ■ Waiting or period signal.

This signal can be made at any time by either the transmitting or receiving ship or station to inform the other station that further communications will follow.

For example, a transmitting ship having completed the

26

sending of a message and having other messages to send could use this signal to warn the receiving ship to wait for further transmissions.

A receiving ship intending to ask for corrections after $\overline{AR}$ had been received from the transmitting ship could also use $\overline{AS}$.

The ship or station receiving this signal should keep a constant watch in order to be ready when signalling is resumed.

$\overline{AS}$ can also be used between groups in a message to separate them (period signal) or to avoid confusion.

CS WHAT IS THE NAME OR IDENTITY OF YOUR VESSEL (OR STATION)?

This signal requires no explanation. It can be made by either the receiving or transmitting station but would normally be made by the transmitting ship.

DE FROM . . . (used to precede the name or identity signal of the calling station).

The use of **DE** will be more fully explained in the procedures used in different forms of signalling.

K I WISH TO COMMUNICATE WITH YOU OR INVITATION TO TRANSMIT

This signal can be used to keep a ship within visual signalling distance or to warn a station that there was a message for them.

It can also be used after the signal $\overline{AS}$, or at any other time, to signify that the ship or station is now ready to receive signals or to resume signalling.

C Affirmative **YES.**

N or **NO** Negative **NO.**

RQ interrogative.

The word **NO** should be used in voice or radiotelephony transmission and when used as a procedure signal should be pronounced as the word **NO** and not spelt out by the Phonetic Tables.

N instead of **NO** should be used in visual or sound signalling.

The uses of the Procedure signals **C, N,** or **NO** and **RQ** apart from their obvious meanings will be more fully explained in the chapter on Coding.

One important point to remember is that they cannot be used in conjunction with the single-letter signals.

It should be observed that **C, N,** or **NO** and **RQ** follow the signal.

Example: **SA** = *I can proceed at time indicated.*
RQ = *The significance of the previous group should be read as a question.*
SA RQ = *Can I proceed at time indicated?*

PROCEDURE SIGNALS IN VOICE TRANSMISSION

It is necessary to emphasize that when used in voice transmission i.e. radiotelephony or loud hailer, all Procedure signals should be pronounced in accordance with the letter spelling table with the one exception **NO**.

It is useful to note that signals on communications appear on pages 91–93 in the General Section YH–ZR in the International Code Book.

NUMERAL SIGNALS

Numbers when used to convey an amount, as for example 5 boats or 20 passengers, are signalled together with the basic group to which they refer and in accordance with the procedure laid down in each form of signalling.

Example: **DI20** = *I require boats for twenty persons.*

Apart from numeral groups representing numbers there are distinct types of numeral signals, known in the revised Code as single-letter signals with complements.

They are distinguished by their alphabetical prefixes or in one case affix which are sent with the figures as one group.

The prefixes **C**, **A**, **R**, may be omitted if the numeral signal can be recognized from the sense of the message.

These optional prefixes can be remembered by the word *car*.

Numeral signals and their prefixes should be memorized. They are as follows:

Azimuth or Bearing Prefix A (if necessary)
Signalled by three figures and given in degrees from North = 000° thence clockwise to 359°. They are always in degrees true unless otherwise stated.

Examples:—
   003° = 3° true, *A*097° = 97° true, 235° = 235° true.

Course Prefix C (if necessary)
Three figure signal given in degrees from North = 000° thence clockwise to 359° always in degrees true unless otherwise stated.

Examples:—
   127° = 127° true, *C*248° = 248° true, 010° = 10° true.

Date Prefix D
Signalled by two, four or six figures as one group prefixed **D.**

The first two figures refer to days and if alone refer to the current month.

The second two figures represent the month.

The third two figures give the year.

Examples:—
   D14 = *Fourteenth day of current month.*
   D0302 = *Third of February.*
   D141260 = *Fourteenth of December 1960.*

Latitude Prefix L
Four figure signal prefixed L as one group.

First two figures denote degrees and the last two minutes.

If near the equator, or if desired, North or South latitude may be signalled by adding to the group N or S.

Examples:—
   L3527 = *Lat. 35° 27 '.*
   L0002N = *Lat. 00° 02 ' North.*

Longitude Prefix G

Four, or if necessary five figure signal prefixed G as one group.

The first two or three figures are degrees and the last two minutes.

In cases where the longitude is more than 99° the first figure of the 100 degrees is usually omitted but it can be included if required.

Where the longitude is near the 180 or 0 meridians, or if desired, East or West may be signalled by adding E or W to the group.

Examples:—

    G1026 = *Long.* 10° 26 '.

    G16523 = *Long.* 165° 23 '.

    G0005E = *Long.* 00° 05 ' *East.*

Note: When a position by latitude and longitude has to be signalled latitude should be signalled first.

    Example:—

    L2335 G3914 = *Lat.* 23° 35 ' *Long.* 39° 14'.

Distance Prefix R (if necessary)

Given in nautical miles.

    Examples:—

    R5 = *Five nautical miles.*

    30 = *Thirty nautical miles.*

Speed Prefixes S = knots.   V = Kilometres per hour

    Examples:—

    S22 = *22 knots.*

    V10 = *10 kilometres per hour.*

Time Prefixes T = Local time   Z = Greenwich Mean time (GMT)

The twenty-four hour Continental method of time is always used so a time signal must always be a four figure signal prefixed **T** or **Z**. The first two figures represent the hours and the last two the minutes from 0000 midnight to 2359.

    Examples:—

    T1415 = *2.15 P.M. local time.*

    Z0907 = *9.7 A.M. GMT.*

Depths Affixes F = Feet   M = Metres
Whenever the text allows depths to be signalled in feet or metres the figures should be followed by **F** or **M** as one group.

Examples:—

20F = 20 *feet*.
17M = 17 *metres*.

K = I wish to communicate with you by (Complements Table I)
This signal is not to be confused with the single-letter signal **K**.

As a numeral signal it must be sent with one figure taken from the Complements Table, as one group.

Example:—

K6 = *I wish to communicate with you by International Code flags*.

All numeral signals may be made by any method of signalling.

The following summary of the list of signals and prefixes will help the reader to memorize them.

Numeral signal	Prefix
Azimuth or Bearing	**A**
Communicate	**K**
Course	**C**
Date	**D**
Distance (nautical miles)	**R**
G.M.T.	**Z**
Latitude	**L**
Longitude	**G**
Local time	**T**
Speed (kilometres per hour)	**V**
Speed (knots)	**S**

MESSAGES

Identity Signals
Identity signals of ships and aircraft are allocated on an international basis. The identity signal may therefore indicate

31

the nationality of a ship or aircraft. A table showing the allocation of these identity signals may be issued by national administrations as a supplement to the Code.

Identity signals may be used for two purposes.

(a) To speak to or call a station.

(b) To speak of or indicate a station.

Examples:—

YP LABC = *I wish to communicate with vessel LABC by* (Complements Table 1)

HY1 LABC = *The vessel LABC with which I have been in collision has resumed her voyage.*

Addresses

Except when otherwise stated a message is always assumed to be from the master of the vessel of origin to the master of the vessel of destination.

If a message is intended for some other individual or destination or originates from some other source the name or names and/or address or addresses should be inserted at the beginning of the text.

In such cases the appropriate procedure should be followed according to the method of signalling used.

The Procedure signal **DE** = *from* can be used when suitable.

Text

This is the actual message and follows the exchange of identities or the address to and from.

In the text a ship may be referred to by her identity signal or alternatively her name may be spelt out.

The names of places are also spelt out. For example:

RV London = *You should proceed to London.*

Time of origin

The time of origin of a message is the time at which a signal is ordered to be made.

It may be signalled as a time signal to the nearest minute and must always be at the end of the text.

Besides giving the time when the message originated times

of origin may be utilized as reference numbers for the messages concerned. This is especially so in messages from ships or signal stations sending many messages on the same day.

For this reason it is advantageous that two or more messages from the same originator on the same day should have different times of origin.

The time of origin could also be used when the time of making out a message is of special importance to the originator or addressee.

METHODS OF SIGNALLING

Now that the preliminary instruction has been completed it will be found that the different methods of signalling are comparatively easy to understand and more interesting to learn.

The few additional procedure signals used in each type of transmission will not be difficult to commit to memory. By dealing with them only in the type of signalling in which they occur the student will be saved confusion. It will be remembered that the procedure signals already dealt with can be used in all forms of signalling where appropriate. They will occur frequently in actual practice.

FLAG AND PENDANT SIGNALLING

Having learnt the flags and pendants of the International Code the time has now come to learn how to use them.

For the different parts of a flag or pendant see Fig. 3.

A brass swivel, in place of the wooden toggle is sometimes fitted.

In flag signalling messages are sent and received by means of flags and pendants. These are carried in a signal locker on a big ship, each flag and pendant being bundled into its own particular pigeon-hole with the hoist and toggle on the outside ready for instant use. Smaller sets contained in a canvas holdall, for convenience in stowing are made for yachts. The halyard by which these flags are hoisted has an eyesplice at one end and if used solely as a signal halyard can have a toggle or swivel seized on to the other end. To make a signal the selected flags are strung together by simply slipping the eyesplice of the halyard over the toggle of the first flag and the eyesplice of the first flag over the toggle of the second flag and so on. The other end of the halyard is secured to the eyesplice of the last flag.

The flags should blow out clear, not be hidden by smoke, and be flown from the halyard best visible to the ship for which the signal is intended. It should be borne in mind that

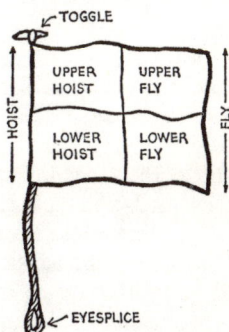

Fig. 3

the receiving ship would have great difficulty in reading a signal if only the hoist or fly of the flag was visible.

If a ship is stopped in a flat calm flags and pendants will droop and be difficult to identify. Sometimes this can be overcome, to a certain extent, by waving or agitating the halyard.

TYPES OF SIGNALS

The explanation that the International Code is divided into groups of different categories will help towards clarifying the arrangement.

Alphabetical groups consist of one, two, three and four

letter signals to which can be added numeral pendants known in these cases as complements.

Complements are dealt with fully in the chapter on Coding and Decoding and need not be studied at this stage.

Each group conveys a complete message.

Numeral pendant groups are also used to signal numbers in the ordinary way. Further there is the list of numeral pendant signals with an alphabetical prefix known in the revised Code as single-letter signals with complements.

In the case of a date signal it is possible to have a group consisting of a flag and six pendants.

ORDER OF READING SIGNALS

One or more groups flown from a halyard are known as a hoist. When more than one group is displayed on the same halyard each group must be separated by a tackline (see Definitions).

When reading a signal the receiving ship reads from the top of the halyard downwards and from the top letter of each group. This order of reading must be strictly adhered to otherwise the signal fails to make sense.

The groups should be written down one under the other so that the meaning when decoded can be written beside them.

Before leaving the subject of the order of reading signals there is one further point to explain.

A big ship can have more than one signal halyard. The maximum number include a halyard at the masthead, two on each yardarm and one or more on the triatic stay.

As a general rule only one hoist should be flown at a time but if more than one halyard is used simultaneously single-letter signals which are very urgent and important or in common use should be read first.

Otherwise the order of reading is immaterial as in the revised International Code each group is a complete signal.

All hoists should be kept flying until answered by the receiving ship.

This pendant has a number of uses and in learning them the reader will gain a practical insight into the working of flag signalling.

It is called the Code Pendant as it is the pendant which represents the International Code.

It is better known as the Answering Pendant as it is in that capacity that it is used.

It is important to remember that it is best not to hoist the Answering Pendant on a triatic stay halyard as if this is done it is difficult to see whether it is at the dip or close up.

The uses of the Answering Pendant can be summarized in the following seven rules.

If the reader fails to understand some of the terms he can refer to the list of definitions.

1. At the dip when the signal is first seen.

It is the duty of a receiving ship on first seeing a signal to hoist the Answering Pendant at the dip as an intimation to the transmitting ship that she has noticed the signal.

2. Close up when understood.

The receiving ship then reads the flags and turns up the groups in the Code book. When she has decoded the Code groups and is satisfied that the signal makes sense, she hoists the Answering Pendant close up as an acknowledgement that the signal has been read and understood. The transmitting ship thereupon hauls down the hoist and it is in order for the receiving ship to lower the Answering Pendant to the dip to await the next signal from the transmitting ship.

3. Hoisted singly close up at the end of a message.

When the transmitting ship has finished her message she hoists the Answering Pendant close up by itself to inform the receiving ship that the signals for that particular message are finished.

37

4. Answered in the same manner.
The receiving ship will then hoist her Answering Pendant singly close up to acknowledge the end of message signal.

5. Hoisted singly first at the dip when preparing to receive in semaphore, and then close up when ready to receive.
This use of the Answering Pendant is fully explained in the chapter on Semaphore signalling.

6. To Signal a decimal point when using numeral pendants.
If it is required to signal a decimal point whilst using numeral pendants the Code Pendant is used for the purpose. Thus the group 2·5 would be signalled numeral pendant two, answering pendant, numeral pendant five, as one group.

7. When a ship of war wishes to communicate with a merchant vessel.
She will hoist the Code Pendant in a conspicuous position and keep it flying during the whole of the time the signal is being made.

SUBSTITUTE FLAGS
It frequently happens throughout the International Code that the same letter or figure has to be repeated in the same group where only one set of flags is carried on board. This problem has been solved in an ingenious manner by the inclusion of three flags known as the first, second and third substitute.

The First Substitute always repeats the uppermost signal flag, in the group, of that class of flags which immediately precedes the substitute.

The Second Substitute always repeats the second signal flag of that class of flags which immediately precedes the substitute.

The Third Substitute always repeats the third signal flag

of that class of flags which immediately precedes the substitute.

Class means either an alphabetical flag or a numeral pendant. In other words a letter or a figure.

In deciding whether a flag is the first, second or third one naturally counts as one reads i.e. from the top of the group downwards.

It is important to note that no substitute can be used more than once in the same group.

It could occur that in a Date or Longitude signal which can have five or six numerals that substitutes could not be used in either the last one or two numerals in the group.

Under these circumstances the extra numerals would have to be signalled as a separate group.

The alphabetical prefix indicating the type of signal should be sufficient to warn the receiving ship that the extra numeral hoist is a continuation of the previous group.

When numeral pendants constitute the class preceding the substitute the alphabetical prefix is disregarded in deciding which substitute to use.

A similar rule applies when signalling a decimal point. Then the Code pendant is not counted.

The following examples will serve to illustrate the use of substitutes.

DD	MMM	MLM	MDD	LABB
D	M	M	M	L
1st sub.	1st sub.	L	D	A
	2nd sub.	1st sub.	2nd sub.	B
				3rd sub.

A225	Z0110	T1122	I.33	
A	Z	T	I	
2	0	1	Answering	Pendant
1st sub.	1	1st sub.	3	
5	2nd sub.	2	2nd sub.	
	1st sub.	3rd sub.		

If an identity signal is not hoisted the signal should be read by all ships within visual signalling distance.

If it is intended to signal to a ship whose identity is known the identity signal of the ship should be hoisted with the signal underneath separated by a tackline.

Identity signals can be hoisted either before or after the signal according to the sense of the message.

Examples:

LABC CW would inform the ship **LABC** that *Boat/raft is on board.*

YP LABC= *I wish to communicate with vessel LABC by ...*

(Complements Table 1).

HY1 LABC = *The vessel LABC with which I have been in collision has resumed her voyage.*

Calling Unknown Ship

CQ = *Call for unknown station(s) or general call to all stations* can be used but if it is desired to signal to a ship whose identity is not known: either of the following signals should be hoisted followed by your own identity signal.

VF = *You should hoist your identity signal.*

CS = *What is the name or identity of your vessel (or station)?*

Bearing in mind the rule that if no identity signal is hoisted the signal should be read by all ships within visual signalling distance, all ships in the vicinity should hoist their identity signals.

The transmitting ship could then call the ship for which the message was intended by hoisting the identity signal of the ship addressed.

Alternatively, an unknown ship can be called by the following signal:

YQ = *I wish to communicate by ...* (Complements Table I) *with vessel bearing ... from me*, followed by your own identity signal.

40

This signal requires a reciprocal bearing in order to discover which ship is addressed.

Finding a reverse bearing is quite easy. If the bearing is over 180° subtract 180° or if under add 180°.

For example the reverse bearing of 185° is 5°: 185−180 = 5°. The reverse bearing of 5° is 185°: 5 + 180 = 185°.

SIGNALS NOT UNDERSTOOD

Although the answering pendant should be kept at the dip, by the receiving ship, until the signal has been read it may so happen that after a signal has been read or decoded it does not appear to make sense. This being so, the receiving ship should not hoist the answering pendant close up but instead should hoist whichever of the following signals is appropriate.

ZQ = *Your signal appears incorrectly coded. You should check and repeat the whole.*

ZL = *Your signal has been received but not understood.*

How to Spell

Names in the text of a message are to be spelt out using the alphabetical flags for the purpose.

In all cases where flags are used to spell out words as distinct from Code groups the signal **YZ** can be used, if it is considered necessary.

YZ = *The words which follow are in plain language.*

The Procedure signals and their meanings used in flag signalling and dealt with in this chapter should be memorized. They are as follows:

CS, VF, YQ, YZ, ZQ, ZL, CQ.

Distress Signal 6—**NC** = *I am in distress and require immediate assistance.*

This is a signal which everyone should recognize on sight when hoisted as a 2-letter code group. It is especially valuable when made by International Code flags as it can be kept flying until assistance is rendered.

5

FLASHING LIGHT SIGNALLING

Calling

The following is the method used to establish communication when using Morse lamp.

General Call (or call for unknown station) $\overline{AA}$ $\overline{AA}$ $\overline{AA}$ $\overline{AA}$ etc. The transmitting ship begins by sending the General Call or the identity signal of the receiving ship if known.

$\overline{AA}$ $\overline{AA}$ etc. can also be made to attract attention when the signal is intended for all ships within visual signalling distance, as a preliminary to sending when further messages are being transmitted after identities have been exchanged or to attract the attention of a ship or station whose identity is not known.

It is sent until answered.

Answering

Answering signal is $\overline{TTTTTTTTT}$ etc.

The answering signal, a succession of T's, is sent until calling stops. It is not advisable to send it until ready to read or write down.

Exchange of Identities

After the General Call has been acknowledged ships should establish their identities in the following manner.

The transmitting ship makes the Procedure signal **DE** = *From* followed by her own identity signal or name. This is

42

repeated back complete with signal letters or name by the receiving ship which then adds her own identity signal or name. This is repeated back by the transmitting ship.

Example:

Transmitting ship's identity signal **GPXZ.**

Receiving ship's identity signal **MNOP.**

After the General Call has been acknowledged the transmitting ship makes **DE GPXZ.**

The receiving ship repeats back **DE GPXZ** and then sends **MNOP.**

The transmitting ship repeats back **MNOP** and continues with the text.

If either ship repeats the identity signal back incorrectly, the other sends it again until the repetition is correct.

Having once established identities they may be omitted in subsequent messages.

If required only the General Call and Answering Signal need then be used.

The Text
The text of a flashing light message can be either in plain language or International Code groups.

Numbers should be signalled by Morse code numerals but they can also be spelt out in words.

It is advisable to do so if the number is of any importance in the message, otherwise the receiving ship can get it repeated if she wishes to make certain that she had read it correctly.

The misreading of a dot in a number can cause a lot of trouble, although there is always the check of the number of dashes.

If the text is in International Code groups they should be preceded by the signal **YU.**

YU = *I am going to communicate with your station by means of the International Code of Signals.*

In code messages names and places etc. will be spelt out in plain language.

Messages not understood

If the message is not understood or, when decoded, is not intelligible the receiving ship should not send **RPT** = *Repeat*. Instead, either of the following two signals should be made.

ZL = *Your signal has been received but not understood.*

ZQ = *Your signal appears incorrectly coded. You should check and repeat the whole.*

Full stop or decimal point

These are signalled by $\overline{\text{AAA}}$.

T ≡ Word or group received

In Morse signalling each word or group sent is acknowledged by the letter T as soon as it is received.

If the receiving ship has not read the word or group, or is doubtful if she has read it correctly, she should not under any circumstances send T, but should wait for the word or group to be sent again and, if necessary, even again until she is certain that she has read it correctly.

Then and only then should the word or group be acknowledged with **T.**

Strict observance of this rule will save much time in getting corrections later.

Erase Signal $\overline{\text{EEEEEEEEE}}$ etc.

This signal must be sent immediately by the transmitting ship if she realizes she has made a mistake in sending.

It is acknowledged by the receiving ship with the same signal i.e. $\overline{\text{EEEEEEE}}$ etc.

The transmitting ship then repeats the last word signalled correctly and proceeds with the rest of the message.

The list of Procedure signals used, where appropriate in all forms of transmission, such as:

RPT, AA, AB, WA, WB, BN, $\overline{\text{AS}}$, CS, OK, $\overline{\text{AR}}$, R, C, N, RQ, will frequently come into use in Flashing Light signalling. For example, the end of all messages, transmissions or signals must be signified by $\overline{\text{AR}}$ which is acknowledged by **R.** Remember **OK** is used to acknowledge a correct repetition and that **N** and not **NO** is used as the negative signal in this form of transmission **C**, **N** and **RQ** should follow the main signal.

The list of Procedure signals peculiar to Flashing Light signalling which should be memorized can be summarized as follows:

AA AA AA etc. General Call.

TTTTT etc.   Answering signal.

AAA   Full-stop or decimal point.

T   Word or group received.

EEEEE etc.   Erase signal.

YU = *I am going to communicate with your station by means of the International Code of Signals.*

ZL = *Your signal has been received but not understood.*

ZQ = *Your signal appears incorrectly coded check and repeat the whole.*

DE = *From.*

MORSE SIGNALLING BY HAND-FLAGS OR ARMS

This form of signalling is only likely to be used if either the transmitting or receiving ship, or both, did not know semaphore, as it is much slower.

It could be very useful to a person who, either through injury or some other cause, could only signal with one arm. The procedure is extremely simple.

Calling

The transmitting ship can either make the signal:

K2 = *I wish to communicate with you by Morse signalling by hand-flags or arms.*

by any method, or the General Call AA AA AA etc.

Answering

The call should be acknowledged by the receiving ship with TTTTT etc., but if unable to communicate by this form of signalling she should make the signal:

TABLE OF MORSE SIGNALLING BY HAND-FLAGS OR ARMS

1 Raising both hand-flags or arms

DOT

2 Spreading out both hand-flags or arms at shoulder level

DASH

3 Hand-flags or arms brought before chest

Separation of 'dots' and/or 'dashes'

4 Hand-flags or arms kept at 45° away from the body downwards

Separation of letters, groups or words

5 Circular motion of hand-flags or arms over the head

—erase signals, if made by the transmitting station

—request for repetition if by the receiving station

Note: The space of time between dots and dashes and between letters, groups or words should be such as to facilitate correct reception

YS2 = *I am unable to communicate by Morse signalling by hand-flags or arms.*
by any method.

Answering each word or group
T should be used to acknowledge each word, as in Flashing Light signalling. If **T** is not sent the transmitting station should make the word again. There is nothing to stop any procedure signals being used if required.

Attention is drawn to the erase and repetition signals in the diagram.

End of message
This will be signalled by $\overline{\text{AR}}$ and acknowledged by **R**.

Note: Both arms *should* be used for this form of signalling, but if this is difficult or impossible one arm will suffice.

The signals used in Morse hand signalling which should be memorized are:

K2 = *I wish to communicate with you by Morse signalling by hand-flags or arms.*

YS2 = *I am unable to communicate by Morse signalling by hand-flags or arms.*
both can be made by any method.

SOUND SIGNALLING

Morse signalling by whistle, siren, foghorn, etc. known as sound signalling is a very slow and somewhat primitive form of communication.

As signals made by these means are likely to be misunderstood by ships other than the one for which the signal is intended, discretion should be used to avoid confusion amongst other ships. Serious consequences may arise if sound signalling is misused.

Signals should be made slowly and clearly.

If they have to be repeated a long interval should be allowed to elapse to avoid confusion. Care should be taken to see that one-letter signals cannot be mistaken for two-letter groups.

The following rules are very important:
1. Except in the case of single-letter signals use sound signalling only in cases of extreme emergency and never in frequented navigational waters.
2. In fog reduce sound signalling to a minimum.

No procedure is laid down for sound signalling. Masters are reminded that the one-letter signals of the Code which are marked *, when made by sound, may only be made in compliance with the requirements of the International Regulations for Preventing Collisions at sea.

Reference is also made to the single-letter signals provided for exclusive use between an ice-breaker and assisted vessels.

SEMAPHORE SIGNALLING

The sender always faces the receiving ship or station.

Calling
A ship or station wishing to signal in semaphore may:
1. Make the signal **K1 (KILO UNAONE)** by any method.
2. Call by simply making the Attention Sign i.e. flapping the arms or flags in the position of the letter **U,** (if the ships are close enough).

The receiving ship can acknowledge the call by:
1. Hoisting the Answering Pendant at the dip and close up when ready to receive.
2. By making the Answering Sign **C.**
3. By making the signal **YS1,** if unable to communicate by semaphore.

If the receiving ship hoists the Answering Pendant at the dip the transmitting ship should make the Attention Sign to indicate where the sender is standing and should make a slight pause before beginning to transmit after the Answering Pendant has been hoisted close up.

The same procedure should be followed before beginning to send if the Call is answered by **C.**

Procedure
Messages—should always be in plain language.

Numerals—should be spelt out in words.

Decimal point—should be spelt out thus, decimal.

Answering sign—each word when read should be acknowledged by C. If the word is not read the receiving station should not send C but should wait for the word to be sent again.

Mistakes in sending—these should be corrected by the Erase Signal $\overline{\text{EEEEEE}}$ etc.

End of message—to be signalled by $\overline{\text{AR}}$.

The use and meaning of the following procedure signals, used only in semaphore should be memorized:

K1 = *I wish to communicate with you by semaphore.*

YS1 = *I am unable to communicate by semaphore.*

C = Used to answer each word.

U = Attention sign, used for calling.

$\overline{\text{EEEEEE}}$ = *Erase signal.*

ADVICE ON VISUAL SIGNALLING IN PRACTICE

To conclude instruction in visual signalling here is some general advice.

In Morse and semaphore most people can send faster than they can read, so never send faster than a receiving ship can read. If you do it leads to inaccuracy and constant repetitions, which in turn make the time taken to transmit the message much longer. The result is more haste less speed.

Begin at a reasonable rate to a strange ship and gradually increase the speed until the receiving ship's maximum rate has been judged.

When receiving a message do not answer a word or group

unless you are certain you have read it correctly. Have it sent again and make sure, if there is any doubt.

The transmitting ship should not wait too long before repeating the word or group. Receiving ships usually answer without much delay. Consequently, if the signal is not acknowledged after a normal space of time has elapsed, it is safe to assume that it has not been read.

It is an advantage to have someone to write the message down when reading.

Finally, when signalling imagine yourself in the position of the other ship and signal as you would like to be signalled to.

RADIOTELEPHONY AND LOUD HAILER SIGNALLING

When using radiotelegraphy and radiotelephony and when using code groups by these methods the Radio Regulations of the International Telecommunication Union then in force must be complied with.

RADIOTELEPHONY

Calling (*coast or ship stations*)

The transmitting ship calls with the identity signal (call sign) or name of the ship called, not more than three times at each call, followed by the group **DE (Delta Echo)** and her own identity signal or name, not more than three times at each call.

Difficult names of stations should also be spelt out using the Phonetic Tables.

Answering Calls

The receiving ship will repeat back the call sign or name of the transmitting ship not more than three times followed by the group **DE (Delta Echo)** and her own identity signal or name, not more than three times.

Once contact has been established the identity signal or name need only be sent once.

Calling all stations in the vicinity

CQ (Charlie QUEBEC) call for unknown station(s), or general call to all stations, will be used for this purpose, but not more than three times at each call.

International Code Groups follow

The word **INTERCO** should be used to indicate that International Code groups follow.

If words of plain language including names, places etc. are in the text they should be preceded, if necessary, by the group:

YZ (Yankee Zulu) *The words which follow are in plain language.*

Waiting signal

When **A̅S̅ (Alpha Sierra)** is used by a station unable to accept traffic immediately, the waiting time required should be added in minutes to the signal if possible.

Figure or mark

These should be transmitted by the figure spelling table.

Mistake in sending

The word or group should be erased by the signal **CORRECTION (KOR REK SHUN)** = *Cancel my last word or group. The correct word or group follows.*

This signal is practically self explanatory.

The receiving station thereupon cancels the last word or group received and replaces it with the word or group after Correction.

Procedure Signals

A list of the four procedure signals peculiar to radiotelephony and loud hailer appear at the end of the chapter.

When using Procedure signals for use where appropriate in all forms of transmission such as **RPT, WA** etc. the letters should be pronounced in accordance with the Phonetic Tables except in the case of the negative signal **NO** which should be pronounced as the word **NO.**

End of Transmission

The end of a transmission should be signified by the signal **A̅R̅ (Alpha Romeo)** which will be acknowledged by **R (Romeo).**

Voice over Loud Hailer

Whenever possible plain language should be used but if language difficulties make the use of International Code groups necessary they should be preceded by the word **INTERCO** and spelt out by using the Phonetic Tables.

Procedure signals for voice transmission (radiotelephony or loud hailer).

Signal	Pronounced as	Meaning
Interco	In-ter-co	**International Code group(s) follow(s)**
Stop	Stop	**Full stop**
Decimal	Day see mal	**Decimal point**
Correction	Kor rek shun	**Cancel my last word or group. The correct word or group follows**

The above should be memorized as should also:

YZ (Yankee Zulu) = *the words which follow are in plain language.*

Signals for flags, radiotelephony and radiotelegraphy transmissions.

CQ = *Call for unknown station(s) or general call to all stations.*

Note: When this signal is used in voice transmission, it should be pronounced in accordance with the letter spelling table.

SINGLE-LETTER SIGNALS

Each letter of the alphabet when made by itself has a meaning and therefore conveys a message. These signals, known as single-letter signals, should be memorized as they are either very urgent, important or in common use. They can be made by the best means available.

They can also be included in a hoist, as a separate group, thus forming part of a message.

Attention is drawn to the note at the end of the list referring to those letters which are marked with an asterisk.

These letters can be remembered by the two words **THIS BED,** which include all the letters so marked.

In the following list of single-letter signals and their meanings an unofficial word or phrase appears with each letter, in brackets, as an aid to the memory.

Single-letter signals have nothing to do with numeral signals which are known in the revised code as single letter signals with complements.

SINGLE-LETTER SIGNALS
May be made by any method of signalling.

For those marked* see note (1) *below.*

A *I have a diver down; keep well clear at slow speed.* (A diver)

*B *I am taking in, or discharging, or carrying dangerous goods.* (Bang)

C *Yes* (affirmative or '*The significance of the previous group should be read in the affirmative*'). (Si signor)

54

*D *Keep clear of me; I am manœuvring with difficulty.* (Difficulty)

*E *I am altering my course to starboard.* (Whistle signal one dot Morse code)

F *I am disabled; communicate with me.* (Flare)

G *I require a pilot.* (Want to go)

When made by fishing vessels operating in close proximity on the fishing grounds it means '*I am hauling nets*'.

*H *I have a pilot on board.* (Have a pilot)

*I *I am altering my course to port.* (Whistle signal two dots Morse code)

J *I am on fire and have dangerous cargo on board: keep well clear of me.* (Jeopardy)

K *I wish to communicate with you.* (Keep looking)

L *You should stop your vessel instantly.* (Lay to)

M *My vessel is stopped and making no way through the water.* (Making no way)

N *No* (negative or '*The significance of the previous group should be read in the negative*'). This signal may be given only visually or by sound. For voice or radio transmission the signal should be *No*. (Negative)

O *Man overboard.* (Oh overboard)

P In harbour. *All persons should report on board as the vessel is about to proceed to sea.* (Blue Peter)

At sea. It may be used by fishing vessels to mean '*My nets have come fast upon an obstruction*'.

Q *My vessel is 'healthy' and I request free pratique.* (Quarantine)

*S *My engines are going astern* (Stern)

*T *Keep clear of me; I am engaged in pair trawling.* (Trawling)

U *You are running into danger.* (U are running etc.)

V *I require assistance.* (Vant assistance)

W *I require medical assistance.* (Wounded)

X *Stop carrying out your intentions and watch for my signals.* (X i.e. Cancel that)

Y *I am dragging my anchor.* (Y am I dragging my anchor)

Z *I require a tug.* (Zephyrs only)

When made by fishing vessels operating in close proximity on the fishing grounds it means '*I am shooting nets*'.

R is not used as a single-letter signal.

Notes 1. Signals of letters marked * when made by sound may only be made in compliance with the requirements of the International Regulations for Preventing Collisions at Sea, Rules 15 and 28.

2. Signals '**K**' and '**S**' have special meanings as landing signals for small boats with crews or persons in distress. (International Convention for the Safety of Life at Sea, 1960, Chapter V, Regulation 16).

Single-letter Signals between Ice-breaker and Assisted Vessels

The signals under this section of the Code, which may only be made by sound, visual or radiotelephony, have nothing to do with the single-letter signals on pages 54–56 with the exception of *E, *I, *S, M, which may be used during ice-breaking operations.

The remaining signals consist of one set for the ice-breaker and another for the assisted vessel.

Example:

Code letters or figures	Ice-breaker	Assisted vessel(s)
A ∙ ━	*Go ahead* (proceed along the ice channel).	*I am going ahead* (I am proceeding along the ice channel).

Signals used, to signify when ice-breaker signals begin and end, are as follows:

WM = *Ice-breaker support is now commencing. Use special ice-breaker support signals and keep continuous watch for sound visual or radiotelephony signals.*

WO = *Ice-breaker support is finished. Proceed to your destination.*

CODING AND DECODING

Construction of the Code

Apart from the single-letter signals the General Section of the Code consists of two-letter signals.

These are listed under general headings in the Contents, page v, according to the subjects to which they refer.

Further it will be observed that each subject has various sub-headings with the numbers of the pages on which they appear in the Code book (see pages 62–65).

The lists of signals with the code groups in alphabetical order will be seen under these headings on the pages given.

For example all subjects listed under the heading Distress-Emergency are between pages 29–47 in the Code book.

The various sub-headings under this section are printed within these pages.

It will be found for example that messages relating to Disabled-Drifting-Sinking are on page 38 under those headings.

General Index

The Code book also provides a General Index, which appears after the Medical Index at the end of the official volume.

In this beside each word is given the two letter code group or groups referring.

The wording of these signals can then be found by turning to the signals in alphabetical order in the General Section and selecting the signal which applies to the message it is intended to send.

In the General Index will also be found the instructions contained in the Code together with the page numbers on which they appear.

Examples:

Addressee
  definitions p2
  general instructions p4
Adrift CB5, DU-DW, RC

Air temperature WV
Anchorage KP, RE-RI, RW, RZ1, ZZ.

Cross References

Coding is also facilitated by the extensive use of a cross reference of signals.

These are signals which will be found also under other headings and can be recognized by the fact that the code group appears after the text on the right hand side of the column.

These code groups can, of course, be used for coding and in decoding they will be found in alphabetical sequence among the lists of signals. See examples of signals **BR2** and **BJ1** on page 63.

Cross references avoid the necessity of having to search through the various headings to find the required message if it cannot be discovered under the sub-heading selected by the person coding.

Brackets

Text in brackets appearing in the text of a signal indicate either an alternative, information which may be transmitted if required and if it is available or an explanation of the text.

Complements

Before attempting coding and decoding it is most important that the student should understand the meaning and use of complements which occur extensively in the revised Code.

Complements are figures added to a basic alphabetical signal and sent together as one group.

They express variations, questions, answers to questions, requests and supplementary information relating to the basic group.

Thus they provide a means of varying the meaning of a basic signal and thereby increase, considerably, the scope of the basic code without increasing the number of two letter groups.

A good example to illustrate this is as follows:

CW *Boat/raft is on board.*

CW 1 *Boat/raft is safe.*

CW 2 *Boat/raft is in sight.*
CW 3 *Boat/raft is adrift.*
CW 4 *Boat/raft is aground.*
CW 5 *Boat/raft is alongside.*
CW 6 *Boat/raft is damaged.*
CW 7 *Boat/raft has sunk.*
CW 8 *Boat/raft has capsized.*

Tables of Complements

Another type of complement is one in which the complement itself has a meaning which can be used with different signals. These are grouped in three Tables, see pages 65–66.

The complements appearing in these tables should only be used in coding as and when specified in the text of the signals in brackets.

For example take the signal:

NB = *There is fishing gear in the direction you are heading* (or in the direction indicated—Complements Table III).

So if it was desired to signal that it was in a south westerly direction the signal would be **NB5**.

The complement 5 means south west, being taken from Complements Table III.

Coding

In the revised International Code of Signals this is very easy.

The golden rule when coding a message is to decide on the subject, or the most important, or operative, word.

Then look up this word in the General Index, where you will find the code group for the message you wish to send.

Alternatively, refer to the sub heading (Contents, page v) of the subject concerned and look through the pages given until you find the code group for the appropriate message.

It should be remembered that the revised Code is so constructed that each group with or without a complement has a complete meaning.

In other words each group conveys a message in itself.

Another point to note in coding is that all signals marked

with an asterisk have a note at the foot of the page and should only be made under the conditions explained in the note or the Regulation mentioned. Some of the signals thus marked will be recognized as procedure signals.

The procedure signal **C** should be used to indicate an affirmative statement or an affirmative reply to an interrogative signal.

The Procedure signals **N** or **NO** can be used to change an affirmative signal into a negative statement and the Procedure signal **RQ** changes the signal into a question.

C, N or **NO** and **RQ** should be transmitted after the main signal to which they refer.

It will be realized that they double the scope of the Code. Examples:

CW = *Boat/raft is on board.* Can be changed into a question by adding **RQ** thus;

CW RQ = *Is boat/raft on board.*

CW1 = *Boat/raft is safe.* This can be made into the negative by adding **N** in visual signalling, **NO** in voice transmission.

CW1 N = *Boat/raft is not safe.*

It should be noted that **C, N or NO** and **RQ** cannot be used in conjunction with single-letter signals.

Communication by Local Signal Codes
If a vessel or a coast station wishes to make a signal in a local Code the signal **YV1** = *Groups which follow are from the local code*, should precede the signal, if it is necessary, to avoid confusion.

Decoding
Decoding is extremely simple as all the work has been done in the Coding.

All that is necessary is to find the Code Group received listed in the Code book in its alphabetical sequence in the General Section or Medical Section and read the meaning, bearing in mind the rules of Complements, Complement Tables and **C, N, NO** and **RQ**.

N.B. Lists of Signals
Although the greatest possible care has been taken to check the examples of signals in the General Section and the Medical Section, to ensure accuracy, the author cannot accept any responsibility for errors which may be present among them.

GENERAL SECTION OF THE INTERNATIONAL CODE OF SIGNALS

(Page numbers refer to the official volume of the
International Code of Signals)
(See Contents, pages v-vi)

Examples of Signals from the General Section of the International Code of Signals

ACCIDENT—DOCTOR—INJURED/SICK

Accident

AK	*I have had a nuclear accident on board.*	
	I am proceeding to the position of accident.	**SB**
	An aircraft is circling over the area of accident.	**BJ1**

Doctor

AN	*I need a doctor.*	
	I require a helicopter urgently, with a doctor.	**BR 2**
	etc.	

Flying

BJ   *I am circling over the area of accident.*

      BJ 1 *An aircraft is circling over the area of accident.*
        etc.

Helicopter

BR   *I require a helicopter urgently.*

      BR 1 *I require a helicopter urgently to pick up persons.*
      BR 2 *I require a helicopter urgently with a doctor.* etc.

PART II ASSISTANCE REQUIRED

	I am in distress and require immediate assistance.	**NC**
	I require assistance.	**V**
CD	*I require assistance in the nature of . . .*	
	(Complements Table II)	etc.

Boats—Rafts

CW *Boat/raft is on board.*

      CW 1 *Boat/raft is safe.*
      CW 2 *Boat/raft is in sight.*
      CW 3 *Boat/raft is adrift.*
      CW 4 *Boat/raft is aground.*

CW 5 *Boat/raft is alongside.*
CW 6 *Boat/raft is damaged.*
CW 7 *Boat/raft has sunk.*
CW 8 *Boat/raft has capsized.*

etc.

Disabled—Drifting—Sinking
Drifting
DU *I am drifting at . . . (number) knots, towards . . . degrees.*

Dangers to Navigation—Warnings
Derelict—Wreck Shoal
MJ *Derelict dangerous to navigation reported in lat. . . . long. . . .* (or Complements Table III).

Warnings
NB *There is fishing gear in the direction you are heading* (or in the direction indicated—Complements Table III).
NC *I am in distress and require immediate assistance.*

Mines—Minesweeping
*PB You should keep clear of me; I am engaged in mine-sweeping operations.

etc.

* The use of this signal does not relieve any vessel from complying with Rule 4(d) of the International Regulations for Preventing Collisions at Sea.

Communicate
ZA *I wish to communicate with you in . . .*
(language indicated by the following complements).
0 *Dutch*
1 *English*
2 *French*

3 *German*
4 *Greek*
5 *Italian*
6 *Japanese*
7 *Norwegian*
8 *Russian*
9 *Spanish*

TABLES OF COMPLEMENTS

Table I

1. Semaphore
2. Morse signalling by hand-flags or arms
3. Loud hailer (Megaphone)
4. Morse signalling lamp
5. Sound signals
6. International Code flags
7. Radiotelegraphy 500 kc/s
8. Radiotelephony 2182 kc/s
9. VHF Radiotelephony—channel 16

Table II

0. Water
1. Provisions
2. Fuel
3. Pumping equipment
4. Fire—fighting appliances
5. Medical assistance
6. Towing
7. Survival craft
8. Vessel to stand by
9. Ice—breaker

Table III

0. Direction unknown (or calm)
1. North-east
2. East

3. South-east
4. South
5. South-west
6. West
7. North-west
8. North
9. All directions (or confused or variable)

GENERAL INDEX

A

MEDICAL SECTION

This part of the Code book is printed on green paper. The Contents are at the beginning of the book on pages vii-viii in the Code book.

It is laid down that medical messages both from the Master requesting medical assistance and the doctor giving advice should be in plain language, if possible, using the text of the Code signals whenever this can be done.

In cases where language difficulties arise Code groups should be used and one imagines this would apply if signalling had to be conducted by flags and pendants.

Referring to the Code, medical signals can be distinguished by the fact that they are all three letter code groups beginning with the letter **M.**

In transmitting and receiving medical messages the Procedure signals for the different methods of signalling i.e. lamp, flags and pendants, semaphore etc. and those for use where appropriate in all forms of transmission are used in the same way as they are in messages from the General Section.

This applies also to the Procedure signals **C, N** or **NO** and **RQ.**

THE CONSTRUCTION OF THE MEDICAL SECTION
This follows the same pattern as the General Section except that the Contents are divided into two parts:
Part i. Request for Medical Assistance.
Part ii. Medical Advice.

The subjects are listed in the Contents giving the pages on which they can be found. See Contents vii-viii in the International Code book.

There is also a Medical Index.

Tables of Complements

There are three Tables of Complements.

Table M I with diagrams is used for coding the Regions of the Body. It is divided into Figure I (front) and Figure II (back). There are also complements for the other organs of the body which cannot appear in the diagrams.

Table M II gives the complements for a list of common diseases listed in alphabetical order.

Table M III gives the complements for a list of medicaments, those for external use in Section A and those for internal use in Section B.

In order to eliminate any possibility of mistake each medicament is described in three ways.

Firstly, by its Latin denomination which enables a correct translation into each language.

Secondly, by the actual translation into plain language.

Thirdly, by a general description of the medicament.

These descriptions should help to avoid mistakes when using the ship's medicine chest.

CODING AND DECODING

Having become familiar with this subject when learning the General Section the reader will find it will present no difficulty as far as the Medical Section is concerned.

The system is the same in both cases including the use of Tables of Complements.

There are however a few points to note.

When requesting Medical assistance the information concerning the patient should be given in the following order:

  (a) Description of the patient (page 102);
  (b) Previous health (page 103);

(c) Localization of symptoms, diseases or injuries (page 103);

(d) General symptoms (page 103);

(e) Particular symptoms (page 107);

*(f) Diagnosis (page 118).

*Diagnosis can be used by both the Master ('request for medical assistance') and the doctor ('medical advice').

It is helpful if this order is adhered to as far as possible.

Certain instructions to the doctor are also given and it is advised that prescribing should be limited to the list of medicaments in Tables of Complements; Table M III.

Another point to be borne in mind when coding from Complements Table M I and when using plain language is that an asterisk reminds those coding to indicate which side of the body is referred to.

When using Table M I the complements are selected by referring to Figure I (Front) and Figure II (Back) but no figure is given for the other organs of the body such as, artery, brain, rib(s) etc., only the organs in alphabetical order and their complements.

Cross References
In some cases single-letter and two-letter signals have a cross reference but only in the Medical Section.

In other words a cross reference will not be printed beside these signals in the General Section (see page 71).

Examples of Medical Section
Examples of the different parts of the Medical Section are given as are also the Code groups and Text of the kind of signals used on pages 70–75.

A study of these should be sufficient to enable those who are proficient in using the General Section to become familiar with the sending and receiving of Medical messages.

Finally, two separate examples of cases are given in the International Code of Signals to illustrate the order in which medical assistance should be requested and given.

A study of these before making out medical messages will be of considerable value. See pages 100 and 101 in the official volume.

MEDICAL SECTION

(Page numbers refer to the official volume of the International Code of Signals.)

Part I—Request for Medical Assistance
Request—General Information

MAF	*I am moving away from the nearest port.*	
	I require medical assistance.	**W**
	I have a doctor on board.	**AL**
	I need a doctor; I have severe burns.	**AN 1**
	I require a helicopter urgently with a doctor.	**BR 2**

Description of Patient

MAS *Patient has been given . . .* (Table M III) *with effect.*

MAU *Patient has received treatment by medicaments in last . . .* (indicate number) *hours.*

Previous Health

MBA *Patient has suffered from . . .* (Table M II).

Localization of Symptoms, Diseases or Injuries

MBF *The part of the body affected is . . .* (Table M I).

* MBH *The part of the body affected is left . . .* (Table M I).

   * To be used when right and left side of the body or limb need to be differentiated.

Part II—Medical Advice
Request for Additional Information

MQB *I cannot understand your signal, please use standard method of case description.*

   Diagnosis

MQE *My probable diagnosis is . . .* (Table M II).

Treatment by Medicaments

Prescribing

MTE *You must not give . . .* (Table M III).

TABLES OF COMPLEMENTS

TABLE M I REGIONS OF THE BODY

Side of body or limb affected should be clearly indicated—right, left.

FIGURE I

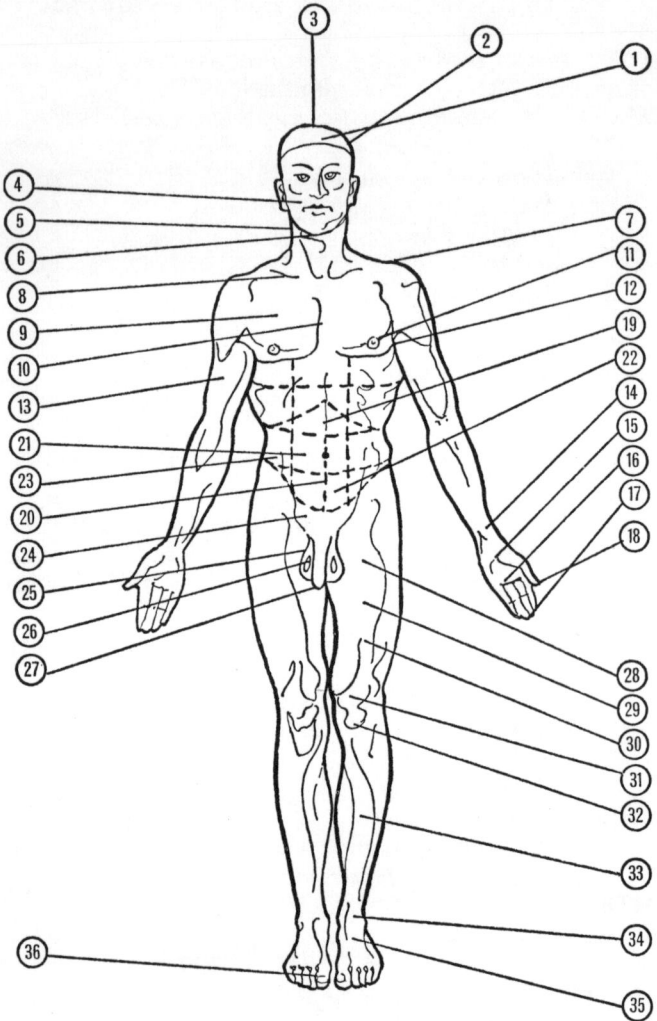

Fig. 4.

Figure 4 (Front)

01 Frontal region of head
02 Side of head
03 Top of head
04 Face
05 Jaw
06 Neck front
07 Shoulder
08 Clavicle
*09 Chest
       etc.

Figure 5 (back)

37 Back of head
38 Back of neck
39 Back of shoulder
40 Scapula region
*49 Lumbar (kidney) region
        etc.
* Indicate side as required.

Other Organs of the Body
57 Artery
58 Bladder
59 Brain
68 Kidney
       etc.

TABLE M II LIST OF COMMON DISEASES
01 Abscess
02 Alcoholism
03 Allergic reaction
04 Amoebic dysentery
05 Angina pectoris
       etc.

FIGURE II

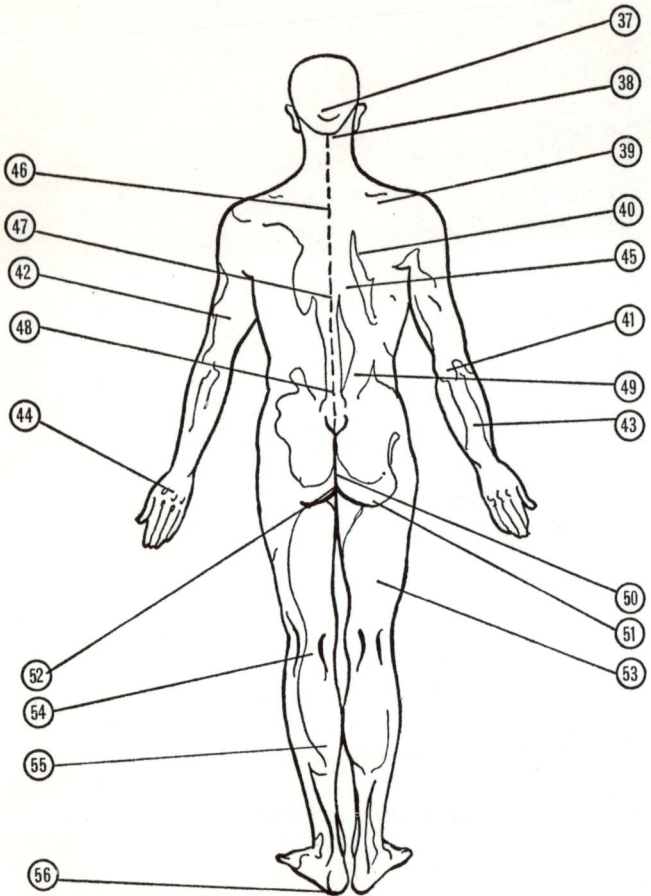

Fig. 5.

74

TABLE M III * LIST OF MEDICAMENTS

A *For external use*

01 *Auristillae Glyceris*
  Glycerin ear drops
  Ear Drops

  * Preparations listed above may have been substituted by equivalent preparations in the ship's medicine chest.

For the sake of uniformity medicaments are indicated in the first place by their Latin denomination so that a correct translation can be found in each language.

B *For internal use*

25 *Linctus Scillae Opiata*
  Linctus of squill, opiate
  Cough Linctus

MEDICAL INDEX

Distress Signals

Prescribed by the International Regulations for Preventing Collisions at Sea (Rule 31).

To be used or displayed, either together or separately, by a vessel (or seaplane on the water) in distress requiring assistance from other vessels or from the shore.

1. A gun or other explosive signal fired at intervals of about a minute.
2. A continuous sounding with any fog-signalling apparatus.
3. Rockets or shells, throwing red stars fired one at a time at short intervals.

75

4. A signal made by radiotelegraphy or by any other signalling method consisting of the group ▪▪▪ ▬ ▬ ▬ ▪▪▪ in the Morse Code.

5. A signal sent by radiotelephony consisting of the spoken word *Mayday*.

6. The International Code Signal of distress indicated by NC.

7. A signal consisting of a square flag having above or below it a ball or anything resembling a ball.

8. Flames on the vessel (as from a burning tar barrel, oil barrel etc.).

9. A rocket parachute flare or a hand flare showing a red light.

10. A smoke signal giving off a volume of orange-coloured smoke.

11. Slowly and repeatedly raising and lowering arms outstretched to each side.

Note: Vessels in distress may use the radiotelegraph alarm signal or the radiotelephone alarm signal to secure attention to distress calls or messages. The radiotelegraph alarm signal, which is designed to actuate the radiotelegraph auto alarms of vessels so fitted, consists of a series of twelve dashes, sent in 1 minute, the duration of each dash being 4 seconds, and the duration of the interval between 2 consecutive dashes being 1 second. The radiotelephone alarm signal consists of 2 tones transmitted alternately over periods of from 30 seconds to 1 minute.

The use of any of the foregoing signals, except for the purpose of indicating that a vessel or seaplane is in distress, and the use of any signals which may be confused with any of the above signals is prohibited.

PART VIII. **International Sanitary Regulations Pratique Messages**

| ZS | *My vessel is 'healthy' and I request free pratique.* | Q |
| | ** I require health clearance.* | QQ |

76

ZT	*My Maritime Declaration of Health has negative answers to the six health questions.*	
ZU	*My Maritime Declaration of Health has a positive answer to question(s)* . . . (indicated by appropriate number(s)	
ZV	*I believe I have been in an infected area during the last thirty days.*	
ZW	*I require Port Medical Officer.*	
ZW 1	*Port Medical Officer will be available at* (time indicated).	
ZX	*You should make the appropriate pratique signal.*	
ZY	*You have pratique.*	
ZZ	*You should proceed to anchorage for health clearance* (at place indicated).	
ZZ 1	*Where is the anchorage for health clearance?*	
	I have a doctor on board.	**AL**
	Have you a doctor?	**AM**

* By night, a red light over a white light may be shown where it can best be seen, by vessels requiring health clearance.

These lights should *only* be about two metres (6 feet) apart, should be exhibited within the precincts of a port, and should be visible all round the horizon *as nearly as possible*.

Radiotelephone Procedures (for Use in Distress)

Name of ship ....

Call sign ....

Reception of Safety Messages

Any message which you hear prefixed by one of the following words concerns SAFETY.

MAYDAY (Distress) Indicates that a ship, aircraft or other vehicle is threatened by grave and imminent danger and requests immediate assistance.

PAN (Urgency) Indicates that the calling station has a very urgent message to transmit concerning the safety of a ship, aircraft or other vehicle, or the safety of a person.

SÉCURITÉ Indicates that the station is about to transmit
(Safety) a message concerning the safety of navigation or giving important meteorological warnings.

If you hear these words, pay particular attention to the message and call the master or the officer on watch.

TABLE 1 PHONETIC ALPHABET AND FIGURE SPELLING TABLES

(May be used when transmitting plain language or code)

letter	code word	pronounced as
A	Alfa	**Al** fah
B	Bravo	**Brah** voh
C	Charlie	**Char** lee *or*
		Shar lee
D	Delta	**Dell** tah
E	Echo	**Eck** oh
F	Foxtrot	**Foks** trot
G	Golf	**Golf**
H	Hotel	Hoh **tell**
I	India	**In** dee ah
J	Juliett	**Jew** lee ett
K	Kilo	**Key** loh
L	Lima	**Lee** mah
M	Mike	**Mike**
N	November	No **vem** ber
O	Oscar	**Oss** cah
P	Papa	Pah **pah**
Q	Quebec	Keh **beck**
R	Romeo	**Row** me oh
S	Sierra	See **air** rah
T	Tango	**Tang** go
U	Uniform	**You** nee form *or*
		Oo nee form

V	Victor	**Vik** tah
W	Whiskey	**Wiss** key
X	X-ray	**Ecks** ray
Y	Yankee	**Yang** key
Z	Zulu	**Zoo** loo

Note: The syllables to be emphasized are underlined.

FIGURE SPELLING TABLE

figure or mark to be transmitted	*code word*	*pronounced as*
0	nadazero	nah-dah-zay-roh
1	unaone	oo-nah-wun
2	bissotwo	bees-soh-too
3	terrathree	tay-rah-tree
4	kartefour	kar-tay-fower
5	pantafive	pan-tah-five
6	soxisix	sok-see-six
7	setteseven	say-tay-seven
8	oktoeight	ok-toh-ait
9	novenine	no-vay-niner
decimal point	decimal	day-see-mal
full-stop	stop	stop

Note: Each syllable should be equally emphasized. The second component of each code word is the code word used in the Aeronautical Mobile Service.

DISTRESS TRANSMITTING PROCEDURES

To be used only if *immediate assistance* is required *use plain language whenever possible*. If language difficulties are likely to arise use Tables 2 and 3 below, sending the word IN-TERCO to indicate that the message will be in the International Code of Signals.

Call out letters in Table 1. Call out numbers figure by figure as in Table 1.

To indicate **Distress**:

1. If possible transmit the *ALARM SIGNAL* (*i.e. two-tone signal*) *for 30 seconds to one minute*, but do not delay the message if there is insufficient time in which to transmit the Alarm Signal.

2. Send the following **DISTRESS CALL**:
   Mayday Mayday Mayday. This is . . . (name or call sign of ship spoken three times).

3. Then send the **DISTRESS MESSAGE** composed of:
   Mayday followed by the name or call sign of ship;
   Position of ship;
   Nature of distress;
   And, if necessary, transmit the nature of the aid required and any other information which will help the rescue.

TABLE 2 POSITION IN CODE FROM THE INTERNATIONAL CODE OF SIGNALS

1. *By Bearing and Distance from a Landmark*
   Code letter A (Alfa) followed by a three-figure group for ship's TRUE bearing from landmark;
   Name of landmark;
   Code letter R (Romeo) followed by one or more figures for distance in nautical miles.

   or

2. *By Latitude and Longitude*
   Latitude
   Code letter L (Lima) followed by a four-figure group; (2 figures for Degrees, 2 figures for Minutes) and either —N (November) for Latitude North, or S (Sierra) for Latitude South.
   Longitude
   Code letter G (Golf) followed by a five-figure group; (3 figures for Degrees, 2 figures for Minutes) and either —E (Echo) for Longitude East, or W (Whiskey) for Longitude West.

Code Letters	Words to be Transmitted	Text of Signal
AE	Alfa Echo	I must abandon my vessel.
BF	Bravo Foxtrot	Aircraft is ditched in position indicated and requires immediate assistance.
CB	Charlie Bravo	I require immediate assistance.
CB 6	Charlie Bravo Soxisix	I require immediate assistance, I am on fire.
DX	Delta X-ray	I am sinking.
HW	Hotel Whiskey	I have collided with surface craft.

Answer to ship in distress

CP	Charlie Papa	I am proceeding to your assistance.
ED	Echo Delta	Your distress signals are understood.
EL	Echo Lima	Repeat the distress position.

Note: A more comprehensive list of signals may be found in the International Code of Signals.

EXAMPLES OF DISTRESS PROCEDURE

1. Where possible, transmit ALARM SIGNAL followed by spoken words *Mayday Mayday Mayday. This is . . .* (name of ship spoken three times, or call sign of ship spelt three times using TABLE 1) *Mayday . . .* (name or call sign of ship) *Position 54 25 North 016 33 West I am on fire and require immediate assistance.*

2. Where possible, transmit ALARM SIGNAL followed by spoken words *Mayday Mayday Mayday . . .* (name of

81

ship spoken three times, or call sign of ship spelt three times using TABLE 1) *Mayday* ... (name or call sign of ship) *Interco Alfa Nadazero Unaone Pantafive Ushant Romeo Kartefour Nadazero Delta X-ray. (Ship) in Distress Position* 015 *Degrees Ushant* 40 *miles I am sinking.*

3. Where possible, transmit **ALARM SIGNAL** followed by spoken words *Mayday Mayday Mayday* ... (name of ship spoken three times or call sign of ship spelt three times using TABLE 1) *Mayday* ... (name or call sign of ship) *Interco Lima Pantafive Kartefour Bissotwo Pantafive November Golf Nadazero Unaone Soxisix Terrathree Terrathree Whiskey Charlie Bravo Soxisix* (Ship) *in Distress Position Latitude* 54 25 *North Longitude* 016 33 *West I require immediate assistance I am on fire.*

LIFE-SAVING SIGNALS

I Landing signals for the guidance of small boats with crews or persons in distress

	Manual signals	Light signals	Other signals	Signification
Day signals	Vertical motion of a white flag or of the arms	or firing of a green star signal	or code letter K given by light or sound-signal apparatus	this is the best place to land
Night signals	Vertical motion of a white light or flare	or firing of a green star signal	or code letter K given by light or sound-signal apparatus	

A range (indication of direction) may be given by placing a steady white light or flare at a lower level and in line with the observer

	Manual signals	Light signals	Other signals	Signification
Day Signals	Horizontal motion of a white flag or of the arms extended horizontally	or firing of a red star signal	or code letter S given by light or sound-signal apparatus	Landing here highly dangerous
Night signals	Horizontal motion of a light or flare	or firing of a red star signal	or code letter S given by light or sound-signal apparatus	

	Manual signals	Light signals	Other signals	Signification
Day signals	1 Horizontal motion of a white flag followed by 2 the placing of the white flag in the ground and 3 by the carrying of another white flag in the direction to be indicated	1 or firing of a red star signal vertically and 2 a white star signal in the direction towards the better landing place	1 or signalling the code letter S (•••) followed by the code letter R (•—•) if a better landing place for the craft in distress is located more to the right in the direction of approach 2 or signalling the code letter S (•••) followed by the code letter L (•—••) if a better landing place for the craft in distress is located more to the left in the direction of approach	Landing here highly dangerous. A more favourable location for landing is in the direction indicated
Night signals	1 Horizontal motion of a white light or flare 2 followed by the placing of the white light or flare on the ground and 3 the carrying of another white light or flare in the direction to be indicated	1 or firing of a red star signal vertically and 2 a white star signal in the direction towards the better landing place	1 or signalling the code letter S (•••) followed by the code letter R (•—•) if a better landing place for the craft in distress is located more to the right in the direction of approach 2 or signalling the code letter S (•••) followed by the code letter L (•—••) if a better landing place for the craft in distress is located more to the left in the direction of approach	

II Signals to be employed in connexion with the use of shore life-saving apparatus

	Manual signals	Light signals	Other signals	Signification
Day signals	Vertical motion of a white flag or of the arms	or firing of a green star signal		In general: affirmative specifically: rocket line is held— tail block is made fast— hawser is made fast— man is in the breeches buoy —haul away
Night Signals	Vertical motion of a white light or flare	or firing of a green star signal		
Day signals	Horizontal motion of a white flag or of the arms extended horizontally	or firing of a red star signal		In general: negative specifically: slack away— avast hauling
Night signals	Horizontal motion of a white light or flare	or firing of a red star signal		

III Replies from life-saving stations or maritime rescue units to distress signals made by a ship or person

Day signals		Orange smoke signal	or combined light and sound signal (thunder-light) consisting of 3 single signals which are fired at intervals of approximately one minute	You are seen— assistance will be given as soon as possible (Repetition of such signal shall have the same meaning)
Night signals		White star rocket consisting of 3 single signals which are fired at intervals of approximately one minute		

If necessary, the day signals may be given at night or the night signals by day

IV Signals used by aircraft engaged on search and rescue operations to direct ships towards an aircraft, ship or person in distress

Procedures performed in sequence by an aircraft			Signification
1 Aircraft circles the surface craft at least once	2 Aircraft crosses the surface craft course close ahead at low altitude opening and closing the throttle or changing the propeller pitch	3 Aircraft heads in the direction in which the surface craft is to be directed	The aircraft is directing a surface craft towards an aircraft or surface craft in distress (Repetition of such signals shall have the same meaning)
		Crossing the surface craft's wake close astern at low altitude opening and closing the throttle or changing the propeller pitch	The assistance of the surface craft is no longer required (Repetition of such signals shall have the same meaning)

84

10

YACHTSMAN'S SECTION

This section has been provided to enable yachtsmen to signal without having to attain professional standards.

The fact that a yachtsman knows that he can communicate with vessels of any nationality or with a shore station gives him a great deal of self-confidence, particularly in times of distress or difficulty.

Indulging in signal exercises for practice with other ships can add to the enjoyment of sailing; naval vessels, especially, will usually be pleased to answer a yacht's signals for this purpose.

The section is divided into three parts:

Part I. This contains sufficient instruction to enable simple signalling to be conducted at sea—by flags and pendants, by Morse and by semaphore—without anyone involved having to know the International Code of Signals in its entirety.

Part II. This is basically a list of selected signals which are likely to be of use to yachts.

Part III. This is a miscellany of International Code distress signals, fog, storm, sound and fishing signals; it also explains lights, cones and shapes.

PART I

SIMPLE SIGNALLING IN FLAGS, MORSE, SEMAPHORE AND R/T

The International Code of Signals consists of a series of one-letter, two- three- and four-letter groups, each of which conveys a meaning which is internationally understood. (The 1934 Code was revised in 1969.)

> *One-letter signals.* Except for R, each letter of the alphabet by itself has a meaning which is either important or in common use.
>
> *Two-letter signals.* Each two-letter signal conveys a complete message.
>
> *Three-letter signals.* These are medical signals and, as such, are outside the scope of this section. Any medical message likely to be required by a yacht will be found among the one-letter or two-letter signals.
>
> *Four-letter signals.* These are ship's signal letters and call signs; they need not be used.

FLAGS AND PENDANTS
Learning
Cut out each of the flags on the endpaper at the end of the book, write the appropriate letter or number on the back of each one and use your set of flags to help you learn the Code.

Aids to memory can be devised: I is like a black eye; V has four Vs in the design; T is the tricolour of France (reversed) and so on.

Size of Flags
Small flags used by yachts for dressing ship are not ideal for signalling; they are difficult to read at a distance and may even go unnoticed. Use as large a set of flags as the halyard will take (remember that there are never more than four flags or pendants in one group and that a yacht would normally hoist one group only at a time).

Signal Hoists

Signalling is conducted in code groups, whose meanings are listed in full in the International Code.

To make a signal the selected flags are strung together by slipping the eyesplice at one end of the halyard over the toggle of the first flag (see Fig. 3, page 35) and the eyesplice of the first flag over the toggle of the second and so on. A yacht will normally hoist one group at a time but if two groups are hoisted at once they must be separated by a six foot length of halyard called a tackline.

A 'hoist' is always read from the top flag downwards.

Substitute Flags

These are used when a letter or a number occurs more than once in the same group; without substitutes the yachtsman would need three or four sets of flags and pendants.

The First Substitute repeats the first flag in the group, so that **NN** is signalled **N 1st sub.**, and **NDN** is **ND 1st sub.** The Second Substitute repeats the second flag, and the Third Substitute repeats the third flag. **NDD** would therefore be signalled **ND 2nd sub.**, and **NDLL** would be **NDL 3rd sub.** Substitutes are used with numeral pendants in the same manner. See pages 38 and 39 for full details.

The Answering Pendant

The Answering Pendant has seven different uses:

1. *Acknowledging*. Hoist the A/P at the dip, i.e. half-way, when the signal is first seen.

2. *When Understood*. Hoist the A/P close up, i.e. to the full extent of the halyard, when the signal is understood. Come back to the dip to await the next signal.

3. *End of Message*. Hoist the A/P singly close up.

4. *Answer to End of Message*. Hoist the A/P singly close up.

5. *Decimal Point*. The A/P is used to signal a decimal point when used with numeral pendants.

87

6. *Semaphore*. If semaphore is about to be sent, the A/P at the dip means preparing to receive; close up means ready to receive. This is usually an elaboration which is not necessary at the normal close ranges of semaphore.

7. *Man of War*. If a man of war signals in the International Code instead of the Naval Code, she hoists the A/P on a separate halyard and keeps it flying; it thus becomes the Code Pendant.

Signals not understood

If for any reason you have read but do not understand the signal which is being sent to you (perhaps the Code book listing all signals is not on board), hoist flags **ZL** which mean 'Your signal has been received but not understood'. If instead you were to send this in plain language by Morse lamp or semaphore, the transmitting ship would possibly reply in plain language by the same means.

Spelling Words

Signal flags can be used for this purpose. The sense of the message will usually show that a word is being spelled; if in doubt begin with the signal **YZ** which means 'The words which follow are in plain language'.

Names of places or vessels are always spelt out in the International Code.

MORSE CODE BY FLASHING LIGHT (ALDIS LAMP)

This is usually in plain language but, if Code groups have to be used, precede the message with **YU** which means 'I am going to communicate with your station by means of the International Code of Signals'.

Learning Morse

This can be achieved in half an hour but speed comes only with practice. Full details on pages 13–18.

Rate of Sending
Four words a minute will suffice but a transmitting ship will reduce her rate until the receiving ship can read it. Remember that everyone can send faster than he can read; so signal accordingly.

General Call $\overline{AA}$ $\overline{AA}$ $\overline{AA}$
The bar on top means that the letters in each pair should be run together and sent as a group. The call should be sent continuously until answered.

Acknowledging $\overline{TTTTTTTT}$
This should be sent continuously as soon as you are ready to receive and until the General Call stops.

Answering Words or Groups
The single letter **T** is used to acknowledge that a word or group has been correctly received. If there is the slightest doubt, do not send **T**, but wait for the word or group to be sent again. Conversely, if transmitting do not send the next word or group until **T** has been received. It may be necessary to send the word or group many times before it is understood.

Numbers
It is advisable to spell these, because the misreading of a dot or dash in a Morse number can cause serious trouble.

Erase $\overline{EEEEEEE}$
Interrupt with a succession of **E**'s if a mistake is made when signalling. It is acknowledged by a succession of **E**'s, and the word or group is then sent again.

Full Stop or Decimal Point $\overline{AAA}$
End of Message $\overline{AR}$
Acknowledge End of Message R

MORSE SIGNALLING BY HAND-FLAGS OR ARMS
This is a method of sending Morse by using the arms. See pages 45–47 for details.

SEMAPHORE

Useful for short distances or if no signalling apparatus is available. See pages 48–49 for details.

SOUND SIGNALLING

Morse can be sent by foghorn, siren, whistle, etc. but there are stringent regulations which must be complied with. See pages 47–48 for details.

RADIO TELEPHONE (R/T) AND LOUD HAILER

Communications are in plain language except when talking to foreigners or when conditions make reception very difficult. In these circumstances the yachtsman may have to resort to International Code groups prefixed by the word INTERCO (pronounced as IN – TER – CO). The letters and numbers of the Code groups are spelt out using the phonetic alphabet and numerals (see pages 78–79). It is worth spending time on learning these.

Calling

Full International Code procedure will be found on pages 51–53 but a yacht is far more likely to call or be called in simple plain language in the following manner: 'Hello yacht Betty. Hello yacht Betty. Hello yacht Betty. This is Niton Radio calling, Niton Radio calling yacht Betty, Niton Radio calling yacht Betty. Are you receiving me? Over.'

Answer

'Hello Niton Radio, Niton Radio, Niton Radio. This is yacht Betty, yacht Betty, yacht Betty, answering Niton Radio. Receiving you loud and clear (or receiving you with some difficulty/interference). Pass your message. Over.'
Once contact has been established there is no further need to repeat call signs three times.

Words of Procedure

There are several procedural words which are worth learning as they make things easier.

Over. I am switching to receive for your next message.
Listening Out. My message has ended, I do not expect anything further from you but I am continuing to listen on this frequency.
Over and Out. This is reserved for the cinema and TV, and has *no* meaning in R/T procedure.
Switching Off. I have finished transmitting and am switching off my radio.
Wilco. I will comply with your instructions.
Roger. Your message is understood.
Kor Rek Shun. (Correction.) Cancel my last word or group; correct word or group follows.
Mayday. This is the international distress call. Transmitted on 2182 kHz, this signal is repeated three times and is followed by the call 'This is yacht Betty', also repeated three times. The yacht's position is then sent three times and this is followed by the nature of the distress.
Pan. A grade lower than distress, it prefixes a message of considerable urgency. A *Mayday* call may be downgraded, to *Pan* if, for instance, the vessel in question gets a fire under control.
Securitay. A grade lower than urgency or *Pan*, it prefixes a message concerned with safety, for instance the safety of navigation.
(If required, full International Code procedure for Distress will be found on pages 77–84.)

PART II—SIGNALS

ALL SIGNALS CAN BE SENT BY
ANY METHOD

Single-letter Signals
Each letter of the alphabet, with the exception of the letter **R**, made individually as a single-letter signal has a meaning which is either urgent or in common use. See pages 54–55 for details.

Two-letter Signals
Apart from the very useful single-letter signals, most of the signals which a yacht will need to know fall within the two-letter group; these are listed in full in the International Code book, but the following is a selection of those most likely to be of use to yachts. The General Index which follows this list is modelled on the one in the official book; it enables the signal required to be found without delay (see page 96).

AC	*I am abandoning my vessel.*
AE	*I must abandon my vessel.*
AG	*You should abandon your vessel as quickly as possible.*
AH	*You should not abandon your vessel.*
AL	*I have a doctor on board.*
AN	*I need a doctor.*
BR	*I require a helicopter urgently.*
CB	*I require immediate assistance.*
CB7	*I require immediate assistance; I have sprung a leak.*
CJ	*Do you require assistance?*
CK	*Assistance is not (or is no longer) required by me (or vessel indicated).*
CO	*Assistance cannot be given to you (or vessel/aircraft indicated).*
CV	*I am unable to give assistance.*
DC	*Boat should endeavour to land where flag is waved or light is shown.*

DV	*I am drifting.*
EF	*SOS/MAYDAY has been cancelled.*
FA	*Will you give me my position?*
GW	*Man overboard. Please take action to pick him up* (position to be indicated if necessary).
JL	*You are running the risk of going aground.*
JM	*You are running the risk of going aground at low water.*
KF	*I require a tug* (or . . . (number) *tugs*).
LN	*Light* (name follows) *has been extinguished.*
LO	*I am not in my correct position* (to be used by a light vessel).
LX	*The canal is clear.*
LY	*The canal is not clear.*
MC	*There is an uncharted obstruction in the channel/fairway. You should proceed with caution.*
MG	*You should steer course . . .*
MI	*I am altering course to . . .*
MJ	*Derelict dangerous to navigation reported in lat . . . long . . .* (or Complements Table III).
MM	*There is a wreck in lat . . . long . . .*
MY	*It is dangerous to stop.*
NB	*There is fishing gear in the direction you are heading* (or *in direction indicated*—see Complements Table III).
NC	*I am in distress and require immediate assistance.*
NE	*You should proceed with great caution.*
NF	*You are running into danger.* U
NG	*You are in a dangerous position.*
NH	*You are clear of all danger.*
NO	Negative: *"No"* or *"The significance of the previous group should be read in the negative".*
PD	*Your navigation light(s) is (are) not visible.*
PE	*You should extinguish all the lights except the navigation lights.*
PH	*You should steer as indicated.*
PI	*You should maintain your present course.*
PJ	*I cannot maintain my present course.*

PK	*I cannot steer without assistance.*
PM	*You should follow in my wake* (or *wake of vessel indicated*).
PP	*Keep well clear of me.*
PS	*You should not come any closer.*
QD	*I am going ahead.*
QI	*I am going astern.*
QO	*You should not come alongside.*
QP	*I will come alongside.*
QQ	*I require health clearance.*
QR	*I cannot come alongside.*
QS	*You should anchor at time indicated.*
QT	*You should not anchor. You are going to foul my anchor.*
QU	*Anchoring is prohibited.*
QX	*I request permission to anchor.*
RF	*Will you lead me into a safe anchorage?*
RP	*Landing here is highly dangerous.*
RQ	Interrogative or *"the significance of the previous group should be read as a question".*
RR	*This is the best place to land.*
RU	*Keep clear of me; I am manoeuvring with difficulty.* **D**
RV	*You should proceed* (or . . . *to place indicated*).
RV2	*You should proceed into port.*
RY	*You should proceed at slow speed when passing me* (or *vessels making this signal*).
SM	*I am undergoing speed trials.*
SN	*You should stop immediately. Do not scuttle. Do not lower boats. Do not use the wireless. If you disobey I shall open fire on you.*
SO	*You should stop your vessel instantly.* **L**
SP	*Take the way off your vessel.*
SQ	*You should stop, or heave to.*
SZ	*Total number of persons on board is* . . .
UG	*You should steer in my wake.*
UH	*Can you lead me into port?*
UI	*Sea is too rough; pilot boat cannot get off to you.*

UL	*All vessels should proceed to sea as soon as possible owing to danger in port.*
UM	*The harbour (or port indicated) is closed to traffic.*
UN	*You may enter the harbour immediately (or at time indicated).*
UO	*You must not enter harbour.*
UP	*Permission to enter harbour is urgently requested. I have an emergency case.*
UQ	*You should wait outside the harbour (or river mouth).*
UR	*My estimated time of arrival (at place indicated) is (time indicated).*
UT	*Where are you bound for?*
UU	*I am bound for . . .*
UW	*I wish you a pleasant voyage.*
UY	*I am carrying out exercises. Please keep clear of me.*
VF	*You should hoist your identity signal.*
VJ	*Gale (wind force Beaufort 8–9) is expected from direction indicated. (Complements Table III.)*
VK	*Storm (wind force Beaufort 10 or above) is expected from direction indicated. (Complements Table III.)*
YG	*You appear not to be complying with the traffic separation scheme.*
YK	*I am unable to answer your question.*
YU	*I am going to communicate with your station by means of the International Code of Signals.*
YV1	*The groups which follow are from the local code.*
YZ	*The words which follow are in plain language.*
ZA	*I wish to communicate with you in . . .* (language indicated by following complements):

0	*Dutch*	5	*Italian*
1	*English*	6	*Japanese*
2	*French*	7	*Norwegian*
3	*German*	8	*Russian*
4	*Greek*	9	*Spanish*

ZB	*I can communicate with you in language indicated* (complements as above).
ZD1	*Please report me to Coast Guard, New York.*
ZD2	*Please report me to Lloyds, London.*

ZF	*I wish to exercise signals with you by . . .* (Complements Table I.)
ZG	*It is not convenient to exercise signals.*
ZH	*Exercise has been completed.*
ZL	*Your signal has been received but not understood.*
ZY	*You have pratique.*

GENERAL INDEX

Use the General Index to find the signal to send.

First consider the operative word or sense of the message and look up this word in the General Index. If, for example, it is desired to send 'I will come alongside', find Alongside in the Index.

Next, find out which of the three signals given under Alongside means 'I will come alongside'.

Direction **QD, QI.**
Distress **NC.**
Doctor **AL, AN.**
Drifting **DV.**
Exercises **UY.**
Exercises signal **ZF, ZG, ZH.**
Fishing gear **NB.**
Gale **VJ.**
Harbour **UM, UN, UO, UP, UQ.**
Health **QQ.**
Helicopter **BR.**
Identity **VF.**
International Code **YU.**
Keep clear **PP.**
Landing **DC, RP, RR.**
Language **YZ, ZA, ZB.**
Leak **CB7.**
Lights **LN, PD, PE.**
Local Code **YV1.**
Lloyd's, London **ZD2.**
Manoeuvring **RU.**   **D**
Negative **NO.**
Obstruction **MC.**
Overboard **GW.**
Permission **UP.**
Persons **SZ.**
Pilot **UI.**
Plain language **YZ.**
Port **UH, UL, RV2.**
Position **FA, LO, NG.**
Pratique **ZY.**
Proceed **NE, RV, RV2, RY.**
Question **RQ, YK.**
Report me to **ZD1, ZD2.**
Routeing of ships **YG.**
Signal exercises **ZF, ZG, ZH.**
Signals **K** (with one numeral) **YU, ZL.**
Slow **RY.**

Steering **PH, PI, PK. PM, PP, PS, UG.**
Stop **MY, SN, SO, SP, SQ.** **L**
Speed trial **SM.**
Storm **VK.**
Tug **KF.**
Voyage **UW.**
Wait **UQ.**
Wake **PM.**
Way **SP.**
Wreck **MM.**

COMPLEMENTS

As explained on page 58 a complement is a number added to certain two letter signals to vary the meaning of the basic signal. The two letters and the number are sent as one group.

There is another type of complement in which the number, itself, has a meaning which can be used with several different signals. These are grouped in three Tables of complements, see pages 65–66.

It is very important to remember that these Tables can only be used with those signals which specifically refer to complements Tables I, II, or III in the text of the particular signal in brackets. See page 59 for example.

Single-letter Signals with Complements

These are sent as one group and are really numeral signals. The letter by prefixing the numerals indicates the meaning of the signal. Thus:

A followed by three figures indicates an azimuth or bearing (in degrees true unless otherwise stated).

C followed by three figures denotes a course signal (in degrees true unless otherwise stated).

D followed by two, four or six figures as one group is a date signal. The first two figures denote the day and, if alone, refer to the current month. The second two figures denote the month; the third two denote the year.

Example: D14 = 14th day of current month.
         D0302 = 3rd February.
         D141274 = 14th December 1974.

F suffixes feet as 20F sent as one group.

M suffixes metres as 5M sent as one group.

L followed by four figures denotes degrees and minutes of latitude (latitude is always signalled first).

G followed by four figures denotes degrees and minutes of longitude.

R followed by figures denotes distance in nautical miles.

S prefixes speed in knots.

V prefixes speed in kilometres per hour.

T or Z. Either of these prefixes a time, using the twenty-four hour clock. T = local time; Z = Greenwich mean time.

PART III

MISCELLANEOUS SIGNALS; DISTRESS, SAFETY AND NAVIGATION

There are other methods of giving and receiving messages at sea, and this section sets forth some of the more important and commonly used ones. It does not pretend to be comprehensive (we hope, for instance, that yachts will not meet many minesweepers actively engaged nor vessels being pushed).

DISTRESS SIGNALS

When a vessel is in distress and requires assistance, the following signals described on pages 75 and 76 are to be used either together or separately. Use of these or any similar signals except for distress is prohibited.

REPORT ME TO

When a yacht which is ocean cruising meets a merchant ship equipped with radio, she may feel that her safe passage should be notified to the authorities. The signal ZD2 means 'Please report me to Lloyd's, London' and may be hoisted or made by other means. Similarly ZD1 means 'Please report me to Coast Guard, New York.'

Shapes

The following may be seen in daylight. The full list is long, but the average yacht will not normally expect to see anything not given below.

Vessel fishing

Vessel fishing (< 65 ft)

Vessel fishing, with gear lying more than 500ft horizontally in direction of cone

Vessel under both sail and power

Vessel not under command (power or sail)

Vessel at anchor (power or sail)

Vessel aground (power or sail)

Vessel towed (if tow longer than 600 ft) and vessel towing

100

Lights

There are many combinations of navigation lights which may be carried at sea; these are complicated and care must be taken not to confuse them with ordinary ship's lights used for domestic purposes. Some of the more common combinations are shown on the endpapers inside each cover.

The basic navigation lights should be carried by all vessels other than small rowing boats, whether under oars or sails (rowing boats shall have ready at hand an electric torch, or other lamp showing a white light, to be used as required). There are certain optional additional lights for sailing vessels (see diagram on endpapers).

Vessels engaged in certain activities are required to carry special additional lights. The more common are also given on the endpapers, but the list is far from being complete.

Sound Signals

Sound signals are used, particularly in limited visibility, to indicate a vessel's presence, type, occupation and intentions. *Types of Signals.* There are several different types of signal which should be known by heart: a yacht may not have to make some of them, but she should be capable of recognising their meaning without reference to a book.

Short Blast. This is a blast about one second long.

Long Blast. This is a blast about 4–6 seconds long.

Whistle. Any appliance capable of producing the above blasts. Power-driven vessels over 40 ft. must have a whistle driven by steam or a substitute for steam.

Fog-Horn. A fog-horn is usually sounded by mechanical means. Sailing vessels over 40 ft. long are required to have a fog-horn; so are power-driven vessels (in addition to their whistles).

Bell. All vessels, power and sail, over 40 ft. long are required to have a bell.

101

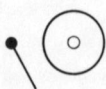

Gong. Vessels more than 350 ft. long are required to have a gong (or other instrument) the tone of which cannot be confused with that of the bell.

Navigation. In clear weather, a vessel will indicate her actions or intentions as follows:

    1 short blast: I am altering my course to starboard.

    2 short blasts: I am altering my course to port.

    3 short blasts: My engines are going astern.

    5 short blasts. You are not taking sufficient action to avoid a collision.

Fog. The following signals are mandatory in fog or any other condition which reduces visibility, e.g. snow or heavy rain. It is of interest that the International Regulations for Preventing Collisions at Sea do not lay down a definition of fog, but the British Meteorological Office state that their interpretation of fog is any condition where visibility is reduced to less than 1100 yards.

1 long blast every 2 minutes. — (2 mins) — (2 mins) —	I am a power vessel under way.
2 long blasts every 2 minutes. — — (2 mins) — —	I am a power vessel stopped.
1 long blast every minute. — (1 min) — (1 min) —	I am a yacht on starboard tack.
2 long blasts every minute. — — (1 min) — —	I am a yacht on port tack.
3 long blasts every minute. — — — (1 min) — — —	I am a yacht with wind abaft the beam.
1 long blast and two short every minute — . . (1 min) — . . (1 min) — . .	I am unable to get out of the way, because I am not under command, or cannot manoeuvre as required or am fishing or am towing.

1 long blast and 3 short every minute — … (1 min) — … (1 min) — …	I am being towed.
Bell run for 5 secs every minute.	I am at anchor.
 Ditto plus gong at similar timing.	I am at anchor and am over 350 feet long.
Ditto plus 1 short, 1 long, 1 short blast.	I am at anchor and you are in danger of hitting me.
3 distinct strokes of the bell, followed by the 'at anchor' signal, followed by 3 more strokes of the bell.	I am aground

If a yacht finds herself in fog without a fog-horn, any method of sound signalling is worth adopting: the sound of a spanner rattling in a saucepan, or coins shaken in a tin, will carry a good distance in fog. If you know where you are, get into relatively shallow water and thus out of the big shipping lane.

INDEX
(YACHTSMAN'S SECTION)

INDEX